Copyright © 2000 John Hunt Publishing Ltd
Text © 2000 Ronald Brown

ISBN 1 903019 72 9

Typography by Graham Whiteman

Write to:
John Hunt Publishing Ltd
46A West Street
Alresford
Hampshire SO24 9AU
UK

A CIP catalogue record for this book is available from the British Library.

Printed in Guernsey, Channel Islands

# FOREWORD

After the publication of *Bishop's Brew* 10 years ago, a number of people were kind enough to send me their favourite story. I also continued with my own collection. Recently I had to make a decision, whether to drop the whole lot into the wpb or share the material with others who might find it amusing or even useful. I hope you think I have made the right choice!

There is an old Jewish saying quoted in the Talmud (c. AD 500): 'The lesson taught with humour is the lesson remembered', and there are good Biblical precedents for getting the point across with laughter. Both Old and New Testaments have countless examples, not least in the sayings and stories of Jesus Himself.

However, humour is more than an effective method of communication. Somebody has said that, next to mystical enlightenment, laughter is the most precious gift and blessing that comes to us on earth. I have a theory that we often laugh at things we disapprove of, and if this collection of stories raises even half a chuckle at the expense of pomposity, greed and humbug, then it will have more than served its purpose.

It is impossible to acknowledge the source of all these quips and stories – 'thou canst not tell whence they come and whither they go' - but I am grateful to those who have contributed in any way. Believe me, the collecting, writing and re-writing have been a labour of love and the book goes out in the hope that church people in particular will, as usual, be able to laugh at themselves and enjoy it. I reckon good clean fun enhances our pilgrimage and ensures we are at least heading in the right direction.

RONALD BROWN

# BISHOP'S BROTH

## CONTENTS

# Chapter One

## THE CLERGY

### (Most Revs, Rt Revs and Rather Revs)

A pushy, over-ambitious vicar phoned the bishop just after midnight. The bishop was none too pleased at being disturbed at such an hour.

'I've only just heard,' said the vicar, 'that the old archdeacon has died, and I want to take his place.'

'Splendid idea,' replied the bishop, 'absolutely splendid: I support it wholeheartedly – provided it's all right with the undertaker, of course.'

\* \* \*

They were on their way home after an important public meeting, the bishop and his chaplain, sitting together in the back of the official car. The bishop was obviously having misgivings about the speech he had just delivered.

'You don't think it was too long ... or too ... boring?' He enquired tentatively.

'Oh no, mi lord,' came the quick reply, 'that thought would never cross my lips.'

\* \* \*

The bishop and the vicar were guests for lunch at a parishioner's house after a special service in the parish church. The vicar was a fanatical teetotaller, and although the bishop had taken a glass of sherry from the proffered tray, he himself turned away in disgust. 'Certainly not!' he expostulated, 'I would rather commit adultery.'

With a twinkle in his eye, the bishop made as though to put his glass back on the tray, remarking, 'I didn't realise there was a choice.'

\* \* \*

One curate to another: 'There are two things I don't like about the bishop – his face.'

* * *

The vicar was anxious to impress the visiting bishop with his pastoral skills, and when a tramp called at the vicarage and asked for help it seemed too good an opportunity to miss. He gave the man a tin of white paint and told him to paint the porch at the front of the church. 'And when you've finished, my good man, there will be a sandwich for you and a couple of pounds to help you on your way.'

The bishop was impressed.

An hour later the tramp was back. With a smart salute he declared the job well and truly done. 'And sure it looks a real treat sir, but you did make one little mistake, for, unless I'm mistaken, it isn't a Porsche at the front of the church, it's the bishop's BMW.'

* * *

A bishop was addressing the school assembly. He said, 'I can remember a school dormitory with seven boys in it. When the lights went out, six boys stayed in bed, but the seventh got out, knelt down and said his prayers. Can you think of anything braver than that?'

One boy put his hand up. 'Yes sir, I can.'

'Well,' said the bishop, 'what is it?'

The boy got to feet. 'I can think of a dormitory with seven bishops in it. When the lights went out, six bishops got out of bed and said their prayers, but the seventh stayed in bed.'

* * *

An organist tells how one Sunday morning his rector told him that the preacher at evensong was to be 'Blind Unbelief'. Greatly puzzled, he listened to the notices with more than usual care. The mystery remained when he heard that the preacher that evening was to be the archdeacon.

Only later did he learn that the clergy had bestowed this nickname because of the archdeacon's tendency to 'err' – that is he had an irritating habit of putting 'err ... err ... err' into every pause and gap!

*       *       *

The bishop's chaplain rushed into the study looking very agitated. 'My lord,' he began, 'the cleaner in the chapel says she keeps seeing a vision of our Lord there. What should I do?'

The bishop said, 'Look busy.'

*       *       *

On one occasion, in the late 1980s, there was an inter-denominational procession in London to mark the inauguration of the Churches Together movement. Robert Runcie (Archbishop of Canterbury 1980-91) walked with the leaders of the other churches. He had been in trouble with a Protestant society and other evangelical groups for what they alleged was his policy of too close co-operation with the Roman Catholics. As the procession made its way to St Paul's, a group of protesters stood by the roadside with a large banner.

'What does it say?' the archbishop asked the Methodist leader by his side.

'It says, "Runcie is a Romaniser",' came the reply.

'Oh thank goodness for that,' chuckled the archbishop, 'my eyes are not all that good, and for a moment I thought it said, "Runcie is a womaniser".'

*       *       *

A bishop received a rather ambiguous letter from one of his vicars. It said, 'Dear bishop, I regret to inform you that my wife has died today. Would you be kind enough, please, to send me a substitute for the weekend.'

*       *       *

A Cornish vicar bought a horse from a farmer who was a very devout Christian. The farmer explained that he had trained the horse to respond only to religious commands. For instance, it would go only when its rider cried 'Praise the Lord' and stop only when it heard the cry 'Amen'. The vicar was delighted to have such a religious horse, he said the magic words and the horse galloped away wildly across the countryside. The vicar, however, began to panic when he saw that directly ahead lay the edge of a cliff with a thousand-foot drop into the sea.

'Whoa, whoa!' he cried as he pulled madly on the reins, 'stop, stop!' But it was to no avail as the horse rushed on at breakneck speed. With only a few yards to go, the vicar remembered his instructions and desperately called out, 'Amen, Amen.' With a grinding halt, the horse pulled up with but a yard to spare. The vicar, mightily relieved, lifted his hands to heaven in prayer and cried out, 'Praise the lord!'

\*     \*     \*

Teacher: What is an archdeacon?
Pupil: Is it the cross on the bishop's neck?

\*     \*     \*

The Pope and the Archbishop of Canterbury were having a game of golf together. While they talked about the game or the weather all was sweetness and light. Things got a bit more difficult on the last nine holes when the topic switched to theology. In fact, by the 18th green a note of acrimony had crept in, so much so that each was claiming to be more like God than the other. They agreed to put the question to the first person they met at the clubhouse. It was at this moment that the local drunk staggered down the path towards them. They asked him which of them was, in his opinion, most like God. He surprised them by saying he thought that neither of them was in fact as much like God as he himself was. 'What's more,' he said, 'I can prove it. Come with me.'

He led them to the clubhouse and they followed him into the bar. They saw the bartender look up from polishing a glass, and say, 'Oh my god, so you're back again.'

\* \* \*

At one period in his ministry, the famous Dean Inge of St Paul's Cathedral received several abusive letters. One that he liked to quote said, 'I am praying for your death, and I have to tell you that I have been successful in two previous instances.'

\* \* \*

After a terrible accident a man was told by his doctor that his leg would have to be amputated. Before giving permission, the man decided to go on a pilgrimage to Lourdes. While he was there he had a vision of the Blessed Virgin Mary, who promised to get St Luke to have a look at it, for 'he was once a doctor and is now very good at arranging miracle cures'.

St Luke came and examined the leg. 'I am so sorry but it really is beyond repair – it will have to come off. However, to ease your distress, I am able to offer you the granting of a special favour, anything you like.'

The man was a keen football fan and had no hesitation: 'I would like Manchester City to win the Cup.'

After a moment's pause St Luke said, 'Let's have another look at that leg.'

\* \* \*

A man throws a bottle of Domestos at the vicar and is brought before the magistrates.

Chairman: 'What is the charge?'

Constable: 'A bleach of the priest.'

\* \* \*

Archbishop Magee was just about to say grace on one occasion when a waiter spilled hot soup down the back of his neck. He struggled to control his temper for a few seconds before saying, 'Is there any layman present who would kindly express my feelings?'

\* \* \*

As the old rabbi came out to rejoin family and friends after an audience with the pope, he carefully crossed himself.

'Oh rabbi, don't say you've been converted.'

'Certainly not! I was just remembering my father's advice to check my belongings when I've been in doubtful company. I was just making sure I still had my glasses, my watch-chain, my pen and my wallet.'

\* \* \*

The rector was very effusive as just before the sermon he welcomed the bishop as visiting preacher. 'We have all been looking forward enormously to hearing what you have to say to us,' he said. One or two people in the congregation noticed he gave a broad wink to the curate as the bishop moved to the pulpit to the strains of *Dear Lord and Father of mankind forgive our foolish ways*. The same people suspected it was no accident that the service sheet concluded with the comment, 'As the bishop moves down the aisle and out of the church the choir will sing *Now thank we all our God*.'

\* \* \*

Dr Whewell, a famous Master of Trinity College, Cambridge, had a deep contempt for the intelligence of many of the undergraduates in the university. He often liked to display this, and on one occasion, preaching in the college chapel, began his sermon on the parable of the talents by saying, 'In this place gentleman, we need only consider the man with one talent!'

\* \* \*

At the end of the cathedral procession came the archbishop followed by his chaplain carrying the primatial cross. It was a splendid occasion, and afterwards a visitor was asked what she thought of it. 'Most impressive,' came the reply, 'but I have one small criticism. The archbishop looked very nice I thought, though if I may say so, I couldn't help but think his wife in front was hideously overdressed.'

\*　　　\*　　　\*

The bishop felt very privileged to be preaching the university sermon in the chapel at Yale. He chose the four letters of the name, Y-A-L-E, and used each one as the initial letter of a key word in his address. Y stood for Youth, and he gave them 10 minutes on that topic. A stood for adventure and another 10 minutes went by. The same amount of time was devoted to Love and then finally to Enterprise. It was all sound orthodox stuff, but sadly, as dull as ditchwater. One young student was heard to observe as he filed out at the end that he was glad he was at Yale and not at the Massachusetts Institute of Science and Technology!

\*　　　\*　　　\*

After his retirement in 1934, Dean Inge took up journalism, and became a very popular writer for the *London Evening Standard*. He once commented, 'I have ceased to be a pillar of the church, and instead have become a column in my local.'

\*　　　\*　　　\*

In 1990, the late Archbishop Runcie was in Liverpool visiting his old school – Coronation Road Primary School. He went in with his chaplain, saying, 'I shall ask one simple question which they can all answer and that will break the ice.'

'We went in,' says the chaplain, 'he took out his crosier, held it up and said, "Now can anybody tell me what this is?"'

There was little response except from a boy at the back who mumbled something. The archbishop who was slightly deaf couldn't hear what was said, so he asked the boy to speak up. The boy yelled out loud and clear, 'Mister, it's for whacking bums.'

*　　*　　*

Lawyers and clergy belong to two of the most ancient professions, and it is claimed they have much in common. For instance, the clergy collect money off the rich and give it to the poor and needy – they call it Christian Aid. Lawyers do the same kind of thing – they call it Legal Aid!

*　　*　　*

An Englishman, Irishman and Scotsman are granted an audience with the pope.

'Is there anything I can do for you?' the pope asks the Englishman.

'Yes, I am nearly blind.' The pope puts the sign of the cross on his eyes and a miracle occurs.

The same question is put to the Scot.

'Yes, I'm nearly deaf.' The pope makes the cross on his ears and another miracle takes place.

'Now what about you?' says the pontiff to the Irishman.

'Keep away from me, Your Holiness,' says the man with some alarm, 'keep well away – I'm on Incapacity Benefit.'

*　　*　　*

Bishop Montgomery Campbell of London (1956-61) was in the vestry waiting for a confirmation service to begin when the vicar presented him with a special request. 'There are four sisters among the candidates,' he said, 'will you please confirm them at the same time.'

The bishop pondered the request carefully, and then said, 'Impossible my dear man, for on this occasion, being forewarned does not make me four-armed!'

*　　*　　*

Bishop Douglas Crick of Chester used to tell the story of an incident when he was Suffragan Bishop of Stafford. It was Sunday morning and he had gone to preach in a country church. As he got out of his car, he noticed that the flag flying from the church tower was at half-mast. He asked the churchwarden about this as they made their way across the churchyard. 'It is important for me to know if there's been a death of someone special in the area so that I can mention it in the prayers,' he explained.

The warden smiled reassuringly, 'Oh no bishop,' he said, 'it's nothing like that. We always fly the flag when a bishop comes to the parish, normal position for the diocesan, half-mast for the suffragan.'

*　　*　　*

A new minister was called to the Baptist church in an American town. He boasted that all the time he needed to prepare his Sunday sermon was during the walk to the church from his house next door. After a few weeks of his ministry, the elders decided unanimously to buy him a new manse – five miles away!

*　　*　　*

Angry exchanges were taking place on the telephone as one vicar complained to another that he had sent him a 'dud' curate.

'You said that you regarded him as a very responsible priest,' complained the first, 'what on earth were you thinking about!'

The other vicar replied, 'Well, during his three years with me, the youth club had to be closed at the request of the police; at least three babies being baptised were given the wrong name; a wedding couple had to hold their reception without being married for the officiating minister hadn't turned up; the church hall burnt down when some fool organised an indoor barbecue; and I myself am on the edge of a nervous breakdown. Believe me, there is no other word in the English language more appropriate for this curate than the one I used – he was, and is, and always will be ABSOLUTELY RESPONSIBLE!'

\*　　\*　　\*

Rather like the royal standard flying over Buckingham Palace, bonfire smoke was a sign that Archbishop Donald Coggan was in residence. (Bishop of Norwich)

\*　　\*　　\*

One of the English-speaking guides at the Vatican got the sack. He was bemoaning the fact, and explaining that he couldn't understand why. 'I was showing a party round St Peter's and telling them what a splendid person the pope was when he suddenly appeared. All I said was, "Gosh, speak of the devil".'

\*　　\*　　\*

Bishop Stubbs (Chester and Oxford) was noted for his witty and terse replies. On one occasion, after an enjoyable banquet the evening before, a friend called at Bishop's House to ask whether he had got home all right.

The bishop was quite indignant. 'Of course I got home all right,' he spluttered, 'it was only my boots that were tight.'

Another time, he had forgotten his academic hood when he was visiting preacher in one of the cathedrals. He borrowed a hood that was not of his university. In the procession he heard one of the canons say, 'Look, the bishop wears a lie on his back.'

He turned and said, 'No sir, no sir, not a lie, only a false hood!'

\*　　\*　　\*

From 1916 to 1936 Lord William Cecil was Bishop of Exeter. Towards the end of his episcopate he was getting very absent-minded. At one of his dinner parties he made sure everyone had a glass of wine except one old lady to whom he gave a glass of water.

'I would prefer wine, bishop,' she complained.

'I'm so sorry madam, but I thought you were a member of the Temperance League.'

'Actually no, I am a member of the Purity League.'

'I do apologise, but I knew there was something you didn't do.'

On another occasion, the bishop was on one of his frequent rail journeys when he was unable to produce his ticket for the inspector. 'Don't worry, mi lord,' said the kindly inspector, 'we all know who you are and that you wouldn't be travelling without having paid your fare.'

'That's all very well,' replied the rather flustered bishop, 'but without my ticket how do I know where I am going?'

\*     \*     \*

The wife of an impoverished curate returned home from a shopping spree with an expensive new dress. Her husband was horrified.

'I am so sorry dear,' said the wife, 'but the devil tempted me.'

'You should have said to the devil, "Get thee behind me Satan".'

'But I did,' replied the wife, 'and all he said was that it looked even nicer from the back.'

\*     \*     \*

Asked about the clergy's ability to teach, one villager said, 'My notion of parsons is that they have a kind of learnin' as lies mostly out of sight.'

\*     \*     \*

It seemed odd that the vicar's son spent most of the time during the meal looking intently down the table, eyes fixed constantly on the guest who happened to be the archdeacon. The vicar's wife could stand it no longer. 'Stop that Percy,' she exclaimed, 'it's rude.'

'But mummy,' replied the little boy, 'you and daddy were wrong, he doesn't drink like a fish.'

\* \* \*

After a sleepless night, the Roman Catholic curate made his way to the bishop's house. He had been summoned to an interview after his parish priest has submitted a very adverse report on his work and conduct. The bishop was a noted disciplinarian, feared by everybody, and the curate rang the bell in fear and trembling. 'I have an appointment at nine with the bishop,' he said to the housekeeper who opened the door.

'Oh terrible news father,' she replied, 'the bishop has died of a heart attack in the night.' The curate mumbled his sympathy and left.

The following morning at the same time he reappeared on the doorstep and again rang the bell. 'I have an appointment at nine with the bishop,' he said.

With a puzzled expression the housekeeper repeated the news of the bishop's death. The curate thanked her and made his exit.

The next day exactly the same thing happened. He stood on the doorstep and began, 'I have an appointment ...' but the angry housekeeper cut him short.

'How many times do I have to tell you, the bishop is dead, D-E-A-D, dead! Can't you get that through your thick skull!'

'I know, I know,' said the curate, 'and I do apologise, but to be honest, it's just that I can't hear it often enough!'

\* \* \*

A priest stays at a hotel during a clergy conference. His bags are unpacked for him by the maid. On the single bed are laid out his pyjamas, on the other his lace cotta.

*   *   *

Mother: It's my experience, Percy, that soldiers and clergymen appeal most to women.
Undergraduate: That settles it. My aim now is to become an army chaplain.

*   *   *

An old bishop left a message for his clergy to be conveyed to them after his demise. In verse it said:
    Tell the clergy when I'm gone
    There is no need for tears,
    For I shall be no deader then
    Than they have been for years.

*   *   *

The Archbishop of Canterbury was on a long flight to Australia. He finished reading the book he had taken with him and asked the airhostess for a magazine. She asked if he had any particular preference.

'Yes,' he replied, 'what about the *National Geographic*?' The hostess apologised for the fact that this was one they did not have on board.

'Very well,' said the archbishop, 'have you a copy of *Playboy*?' Again the answer was in the negative, but the hostess was curious at the request for two such totally different magazines and she asked him why this was so.

'Oh it's quite simple really,' retorted the archbishop, 'it's just that I love looking at the places I'm never likely to go to.'

*   *   *

There was some confusion in a Welsh parish at one time when both curates bore the name of Evans. The difficulty was short-lived however, for before long one was known as Evans the Trinity, and the other as Evans the Holy Ghost. Both men were flattered when they discovered this, until it was revealed that they had been dubbed thus because one was incomprehensible and the other generally invisible. The confusion was compounded when the new rector arrived, for he too had the same name. But that was even more easily sorted – from the very first day he was, of course, Evans Above.

\*　　\*　　\*

A joke that goes the rounds of the Roman Catholic Church tells how bishops are appointed. There are apparently three conditions for being made an RC bishop in England. The candidate must be:
- Male
- Baptised
- A former student of the English College in Rome

It is said that in exceptional circumstances, the first two conditions may be dispensed with!

\*　　\*　　\*

Parishioner: Did you wake up grumpy this morning?
Vicar's wife: No, I thought I would let him sleep on.

\*　　\*　　\*

Two Liverpudlians are sitting together on a bus when a man with a white beard gets on and sits at the back.

'That's the pope,' says one.

'Never,' says the other.

'Bet you. I'll go and ask him, and you'll see I'm right.'

He goes off to the back of the bus and puts the question: 'Are you the pope?'

'Clear off, you idiot – go on, get lost!'

He asks again. 'No, I mean, are you the pope?'
'If you don't scram, I'll knock yer teeth in!'
He gives up and goes back to his companion.
'Well?'
'Don't know, he wouldn't tell me.'

\*　　\*　　\*

The dean's wife was a remarkable woman who even during her pregnancy had written a distinguished book. Baby and book appeared at about the same time, and the dean was inordinately proud of both. One of the canons congratulated him on the arrival of his son and heir, but the dean was obviously focused on his wife's literary efforts.

'We are all very pleased,' said the canon.

'Thank you, thank you,' enthused the dean, 'and I want you all to know I've had nothing to do with it, though I suspect the archdeacon may have had a hand in it.'

\*　　\*　　\*

It was said of William Howley (Archbishop of Canterbury 1828-48) that his speeches in the House of Lords were completely incomprehensible. And certainly, in 1837 when he went to congratulate Victoria on her accession to the throne and to pray with her, he had to be reminded of the reason for his visit.

\*　　\*　　\*

After announcing his retirement, a vicar received several letters from removal firms in the area asking to be allowed to tender for the job of taking the priest's furniture to his new home. One of these letters boasted, 'In the past few years we have removed more than a dozen clergymen from this area to the complete satisfaction of all concerned.'

\*　　\*　　\*

The pope had an urgent letter for his clergy, so of course he sent it FAX VOBISCUM.

*     *     *

Frederick Temple, Archbishop of Canterbury 1896-1903, was free of official duties one Sunday morning and went unannounced to the parish church in the vicinity of his residence. At the end of the service, the vicar stood by the door saying goodbye to everyone. As the archbishop left, the vicar explained that it had been a perfectly normal Sunday morning service – 'Nothing special, your grace, even though I did spot you in the congregation. And my sermon was just my usual little talk, for nowadays I never prepare anything, I just say what comes into my head. I've been preaching like this for quite a few years now, in fact ever since one Sunday when I forgot my notes and had to give an impromptu address. It seemed so good to me that I took a vow that day that I would never prepare or use notes again.'

The archbishop drew himself up to his full height, and in his deep bass voice loudly declared, 'I Frederick, by Divine Providence Archbishop of Canterbury, Primate of all England and Metropolitan, do hereby on this Sabbath day, solemnly and finally absolve thee from thy vow, from this time forth and for evermore. Amen.'

*     *     *

Getting rid of an unsatisfactory curate can be quite a problem for a vicar. It is often necessary to try to get him another position in a different diocese where he is unknown and can make a fresh start. This is known in the trade as 'throwing dead cats over the boundary fence'! Sometimes the vicar has to 'gild the lily' a bit as he writes the reference, with a touch of ambiguity here and there, as for instance when trying to hasten the departure of a work-shy colleague. Phrases like the following are not unknown:

I can assure you, a curate like this is hard to find.

He will not do anything that will lower your high regard for him.

He has worked in this parish more or less for a year.

He is definitely a young man to watch.

As to whether he needs supervision, I can say he generally works without any direction.

\* \* \*

Graham Leonard on being Bishop of London: 'It is like wrestling with a lubricated jellyfish.'

\* \* \*

Difficult as it is to find the right name for a child, it can be even more of a challenge to find a suitable name for a house. There have been some valiant attempts. A council house tenant came up with 'Tain Towers', and others worthy of note are 'Suitsus', 'Thisledoo', and 'Kumincyde'. For retirement homes you can find an old favourite like 'Dunromin', or you can have a name that hints at the former profession of the owner, like 'Copper Leaves' (former policeman) or 'Aftermath' (maths teacher), and of course 'Vicaraged' speaks for itself.

\* \* \*

One of the most caustic bishops of modern times has been Douglas Feaver of Peterborough (1972-84). When a woman misspelt his name as Fever, she got a reply which said, 'Madam, I am not now, nor have I ever been a disease!'

Once the bishop was with other dignitaries in a church porch waiting for the procession to begin at the commencement of an induction service. A young curate in the diocese had been given the role of bishop's chaplain, and to break the rather uncomfortable silence, he blurted out, 'By the way bishop, we've got a new baby at our house this week.'

The bishop looked at the others with raised eyebrows and enquired archly, 'Anybody here ever heard of an *old* baby?'

In the same vein, he squashed a rather pompous man at

a reception one day when the man pushed forward and said, 'My lord, may I introduce my dear little wife.'

'Presumably,' replied the bishop, 'you've left the larger one at home.'

At his retirement party, the clergy presented him with a cheque. In thanking them he said, 'With this I shall buy a carpet for the study in my new home, and every time I walk on it I shall think of the clergy of this diocese.'

Before he actually left the diocese he was interviewed on local radio. In response to the question, 'What would you have liked to have done that you haven't been able to do in the 12 years of your episcopate?' he answered without hesitation, 'Bury a few people I would dearly have loved to.'

\*      \*      \*

Insults can flow the other way too, often in the form of backhanded compliments, as a bishop found when he was guest speaker at a rotary club dinner.

'Do you wish the bishop to speak now, or would you like to enjoy yourselves a little bit longer?' enquires the chairman as he interrupts the hubbub at the end of the meal. He then makes the introduction. 'Anyone who has ever heard him speak will appreciate why we have invited him as our guest speaker tonight. I am sure you will enjoy his debatable qualities, and find his speech as moving as the food has been.'

\*      \*      \*

There were two official dinner parties taking place in the same hotel on the same evening. One was for a group of businessmen in the area, and the other for a party of evangelical clergymen who all happened to be rabid teetotallers. The chef had designed the same menu for both groups with the exception of the starter: the businessmen were to have port melon while the clergymen were to have vegetable soup. Alas, an inexperienced waiter served the starters the wrong way round. The manager was horrified, and asked the waiter if there had been any complaints. He was reassured when he was told, 'No, nobody seemed to notice, though I must say I thought it rather strange that quite a few of the clergy at the end asked me if they could have some of the melon seeds to take home.'

*     *     *

It was in the mid-70s that George Reindorp, Bishop of Salisbury, went out as usual on Sunday morning to conduct a service at a small country church in his diocese. It was a particularly windy day, and because of this the bishop left home much earlier than he would normally have done, and as a consequence arrived very early at the church gates. He sat in his car for a while and then decided he would be warmer and more comfortable inside. However, he found the main door locked and made his way round to what he presumed would be the vestry door. It was then that he heard noises coming from within. As well as voices, there were sounds of bangings and scrapings as furniture was moved around. He knocked loudly on the door several times before being greeting with, 'B****r off, we're busy.'

He knocked again even louder, only to be asked once more to depart in the same unambiguous fashion, but this time he was at least given an explanation – 'We're expecting the b****y bishop.'

With a final couple of knocks, George Reindorp, in his loudest voice, proclaimed, 'I am the b****y bishop!'

He says a strange, eerie silence followed, broken finally by two words that might have been the beginning of a prayer, 'Oh Lord!'

*     *     *

Geoffrey Fisher made a name for himself as Archbishop of Canterbury (1945-61) by . bringing about some very necessary administrative reforms, including the mammoth task of the revision of Canon Law. He himself was a model of efficiency and administrative order. It is said that on completing the reading of a lesson at a bishop's meeting at

Lambeth, instead of saying, 'Here endeth the first lesson', he actually said, 'Yours sincerely, Geoffrey Cantuar'.

Once he asked a group of children what *Cantuar* meant. 'Is it half horse, half man?' queried a little girl. The archbishop replied, 'Wrong answer, but a good job description.'

\*     \*     \*

Isaac goes to his local rabbi in despair and tells him that his son wants to be baptised.

'Well,' says the rabbi, 'look at my own son.'

'You don't mean your own son, rabbi, wants to be baptised?'

'Yes, that is exactly what I do mean.'

'And what have you done about it?'

'What can a rabbi do but turn to God?'

'And what did God say to you?'

'God said to me exactly what I said to you – "Look at my own Son".'

\*     \*     \*

A small boy was watching his father being consecrated bishop in York Minster. He had not been told how he would be surrounded by the other bishops for the imposition of hands. He was quite alarmed when his father seemed to disappear in the midst of them.

'Whatever are they doing to daddy?' he asked.

His mother was quick to reassure him. 'Don't worry dear, they are merely removing his backbone.'

\*     \*     \*

An old farmer attended his first meeting of the diocesan synod, and was asked for his impressions. 'It's confirmed what I've always thought,' he said, 'I think the clergy are like manure, very beneficial when spread out thin over a wide area, but not very pleasant when found in a heap.'

\*     \*     \*

Everybody knew the dean had outstayed his welcome. He had done splendid work for a long period, but now after 30 years he was clearly past it. Even the kindly bishop had been heard to remark, 'The dean has every Christian virtue except that of resignation.'

\*     \*     \*

During a visit to the Vatican, an American bishop noticed that there were two telephones on the pope's desk, one red and the other white. His Holiness explained that the red phone was the ordinary one, but the white one was a direct line to God. The visitor asked if he could use it and was told that the cost was a hundred dollars a minute. He accepted and made his call. A few days later the bishop had moved on to Jerusalem and was received by the prime minister. He saw that exactly the same types of phones were on his desk, and he asked if he could use the white one. The PM agreed and said that the cost would be five dollars a minute.

'But how is it that the same call in Rome is so much more expensive?' he asked.

He was told, 'Well you see bishop, from here it's just a local call.'

\*     \*     \*

The bishop was introduced to the meeting in such glowing terms that he began his speech by saying, 'I feel I should begin by saying two prayers – one for the chairman who has told so many lies, and the other for myself who has so much enjoyed hearing them.'

\*     \*     \*

Little girl: 'Mummy, when we are in church, why do we ask God to eliminate all bishops, priests and deacons?'

\*     \*     \*

The bishop was explaining the working of the Church of England to a member of another denomination. He says, 'On many issues the General Synod is of one mind – incredible isn't it, 600 members and just one mind.'

*     *     *

An elderly, rotund bishop was returning home across a marshy field when his feet started to sink under him. One of the bystanders spotted the danger and with a 999 call summoned the fire brigade. When it arrived, the bishop waved it away, saying, 'Don't worry, God will take care of me.'

However, as he trudged on, his feet sank deeper and deeper and the fire brigade was re-called. Once again the bishop airily dismissed it, and at the same time admonished the bystanders for their lack of faith in divine protection. A few minutes later the bishop sank from sight. He awoke in heaven and at once demanded an interview with God. 'How could you let me down like that,' he moaned, 'and in front of all those unbelievers.'

'Let you down!' came the reply, 'don't you realise I even sent the fire brigade twice.'

*     *     *

# Chapter Two

## THE SERVICES

### All Things Bright and Hootiful

An old lady from the North-East of England tells the true story of an incident that happened many years ago. They had at their church a very bossy verger who liked to rule the roost. One Sunday morning he stood just inside the door and watched with growing concern as an elderly lady fitted together one of those old-fashioned ear trumpets. The verger decided it was his duty to intervene, and going over he tapped her on the shoulder, and in his broad Northumbrian dialect gave a grave warning, 'Noo hinney, one toot and you're oot.'

*　　*　　*

When the collection plate came round, Charlie put on a fiver. Later in the service there was a special collection for the victims of a famine in Africa, and again his wallet came out. After the blessing the vicar appealed for donations to the organ fund and said there would be a plate at the back. When Charlie got to the door, instead of shaking hands with the vicar, he lifted both hands above his head and said, 'Go on vicar, I expect you'll want to frisk me before you let me go.'

*　　*　　*

An old lady fainted during the Eucharist. They carried her into the porch where she quickly revived. She was full of apologies. 'I am so very sorry,' she said, 'but I always feel faint when we have incest in the service.'

*　　*　　*

The churchwarden was rather overawed at having to make the speech after the service thanking the bishop for his visit.

However, it seemed to go quite well, though it was thought he could have ended it better than by saying. 'And finally, I can honestly say that when you finished your sermon, mi lord, some of us felt there was a great awakening in the congregation.'

*     *     *

Suddenly the vicar's sermons got much better and everybody was pleased. After a couple of months of this improved fare, one of the churchwardens was bold enough to comment on it. 'Vicar,' he said, 'your sermons have been appreciated much more in recent weeks, in fact ever since you started them by raising your arms high above your head and wriggling your fingers. Is this a charismatic way of seeking God's assistance?'

'Gosh no,' replied the cleric, 'I'm simply being honest and using quotation marks.'

*     *     *

What most people pray for when they arrive at church on a Sunday is a parking place!

*     *     *

Following a well-established tradition, Manny allows the Jewish matchmaker to try to find him a prospective bride. But when he turns up for his first meeting with the intended, he is absolutely horrified.

He complains vigorously to the broker. 'How could you do this to me?' he whispers, 'Just look at her, she is cross-eyed, nearly bald, has bad teeth, and must weigh 15 stone.'

'No need to whisper,' replies the broker, 'she's deaf as well.'

*     *     *

The vicar had been known to quibble at certain names being suggested for the baby before a baptism. He had refused point-blank to accept 'Hill Forty', even though this was said to be the military position of the father in the desert when the child was born. In the 25th year of the Queen's reign he refused to let Mr and Mrs Lee call their daughter Juby, and it goes without saying that had Mrs Down wanted her son called Neil, or Mrs Button opted for Pearl for her daughter, or Mrs Bloomer Georgette, they would have met with a similar response. It would also have been of no avail for Mr and Mrs Carte to claim that they were great fans of film-star Orson Welles, had they wanted to name their son after him, and the vicar would no doubt have had an apoplectic fit had Mr and Mrs White requested the name Isla for their baby daughter!

\*       \*       \*

I suspected my new mother-in-law didn't like me very much when I saw her bite the head off the miniature bridegroom on the wedding cake.

\*       \*       \*

A true story comes from a parish near Wigan in the 1920s. Although the miners as a whole seldom went to church, they generally liked to support the children on the Sunday School Anniversary Sunday. Many of them used to hurry back to the pub for a pint when the service was over. One year, George was back in the pub standing by the bar, glass in hand, but looking decidedly miserable. 'What's matter, George,' asked a friend, 'didn't you enjoy t'service?'

'Aye, I enjoyed it reet enough,' George replied, 'but when it was collection, I went to put a bob on t'plate but got wrong pocket and put in sovereign instead.'

'Well, never mind, they'll still be counting t'collection in t'vestry, and they'll understand and give it thee back.'

George downed his pint and headed back to the church. At the door his courage failed him, and after standing on shifting feet for a full five minutes, he returned to the bar. His friend was still there. George spoke to him: 'Changed mi mind,' he said, 'Ah gave it to the Lord, and to hell with it.'

*     *     *

Doddery old priest beginning evensong: 'Let us confess our sins in the words of the General Thanksgiving.'

*     *     *

It was reported to the vicar that during the sermon the curate had stood on his head in the pulpit, done a conjuring trick, told half a dozen jokes and juggled three oranges. The vicar was furious. 'That's the last funeral I will ever let him take in this parish,' he said.

*     *     *

Misprint on carol sheet: 'The palmist foretells the wonders of Christ's kingdom.'

*     *     *

Mark Twain always enjoyed a good leg-pull. One Sunday morning, as he went out of church at Hartford, he congratulated the Rector, Dr Doane, on his splendid sermon. But with a twinkle in his eye he added, 'However, I do happen to know that every word of it came from a book I've got at home.'

When the rector indignantly denied it, Mark Twain said, 'Very well, I'll send you the book as soon as I get home.' In a short time a messenger arrived at the rectory with a copy of Webster's *American Dictionary of the English Language*!

*     *     *

An English vicar, an Irish priest and a Scottish minister were discussing how they disposed of their church collection on a Sunday. The English vicar said, 'I keep the small change for my expenses but the silver and the notes go into the church account for God's work in the parish.'

The Irish priest said, 'Since I have no other source of

income, I put aside all the copper and silver for God, but the notes I keep for myself.'

The Scottish minister said, 'I try to deal with this business in a more religious way than either of you. On a Sunday night I put the day's collection in a blanket and then toss the whole lot in the air. God keeps what he wants and throws the rest down to me.'

\*        \*        \*

We are told that most girls marry men who resemble their fathers. Probably this is why mothers generally cry at weddings.

\*        \*        \*

The little girl seemed to get more and more bored during the lengthy service. There were several yawns and sighs. Finally she fixed her eyes on the red sanctuary lamp and said hopefully, 'Mummy, when the light changes to green, can we go.'

\*        \*        \*

Mrs Rafferty never did like the curate and delighted in the opportunity to show him up when he made mistakes in his sermons, which he often did because he was so very nervous in the pulpit. On one occasion he said that Jesus had fed a great crowd with five thousand loaves and two thousand fishes. From the congregation Mrs Rafferty called out, 'Even I could do that!'

Ruffled somewhat, the curate ploughed on, and it was only later that someone explained what he had actually said. The next Sunday came his opportunity to apologise and put matters right.

Do forgive me,' he pleaded, 'I should of course have said that Jesus fed the five thousand with five loaves and two small fishes.'

Once again Mrs Rafferty saw her opportunity, and for the second time in two weeks interrupted the sermon with the cry, 'Even I could do that!'

'Really Mrs Rafferty,' said the embarrassed young man, 'how could you possibly do that?'

Quick as a flash came the answer: 'With what you had left over from last week, that's how!'

*     *     *

'I hope you will be very happy,' said the vicar to the bridegroom in the vestry after the wedding.

'I don't see why not,' came the reply, 'I came through the war alright.'

*     *     *

Ecclesiastical Strine:

It was Monica Dickens in the 1960s who stumbled across the language known as Strine (ie Australian). She was in a Sydney bookshop signing copies of her latest book when a woman walked up and said 'Emma Chisit'. Thinking this was her name, Miss Dickens wrote on the flyleaf, 'To Emma Chisit'.

The customer didn't like it and howled, 'No, no, Emma Chisit'. Fortunately the shop assistant was fluent in Strine and translated, 'How much is it?'

It is said that there is now a professor of Strine at Sinny University, and so help is available for translation of phrases sometimes even heard in churches, such as Gloria Soame (glorious home) and marmon dead (mum and dad): a preacher was heard to say that some contemporaries of Jesus thought that he was orpheus rocker (unstable), and one of the most popular hymns at Australian weddings is Big Horse Cart Major Mine (*Because God made you mine*).

*     *     *

Paddy was told he had to take his car for its first service. Unfortunately he ran into the pulpit!

*   *   *

The old rector left a one-word piece of advice in the pulpit for the new curate. In large letters on the pulpit desk was the word *KISS*.

'Oh sir,' said the rather wet young man, 'what a lovely idea, I like it. You must mean that I am to blow a kiss to the whole congregation, rather like the "kiss of peace" in the old liturgies.'

'Rubbish,' growled the old priest, 'it means, *Keep it Simple, Stupid!*'

*   *   *

The vicar complained, 'I find that when I'm taking a service, the only people willing to come to the front of the church are escorted by pallbearers.'

*   *   *

The preacher was emphasising the need for mutual forgiveness. 'None of us is perfect,' he thundered, 'does anybody in this church today think he's perfect? If anybody thinks he's perfect, let him stand up right now in front of us all.' There was silence for a moment, and then to the preacher's astonishment a man in the front pew got to his feet.

'Do you honestly think you are perfect?' the preacher enquired incredulously.

'Oh no, not me,' said the man, 'I'm standing here proxy for my wife's first husband.'

*   *   *

Francis Kilvert, in his diary, described his life as curate and vicar in the 1870s. Two stories from those days concern the two great sacraments. At Holy Communion a farm labourer kneeling at the rail took the chalice from the vicar, raised it high and said, 'I drinks your 'ealth sir'. Further along the line another parishioner tried to improve on this with 'I drinks your 'ealth, Lord Christ'.

The other story concerns Baptism. Kilvert tells of a new vicar in a neighbouring parish who asked his verger to bring water so that he could administer the sacrament.

'Water sir? Water!' said the surprised verger, 'previous parson just used to spit on our 'eads.'

\*       \*       \*

The local newspaper had a rather sensational caption under one of its wedding photographs: *The bride and groom are seen here leaping the parish church after the ceremony.*

\*       \*       \*

A woman stopped going to evensong in the parish church. She said this was because there were so few people present that when the vicar addressed the congregation as 'Dearly beloved', she blushed and felt embarrassed.

\*       \*       \*

The American visitor to morning prayer in the parish church was deeply moved by the vicar's passionate appeal for help to repair the church roof. He responded at once with a very generous gift.

However, after being present at evensong that same day, he hurried back to his hotel determined to phone the bank at the first opportunity to cancel the cheque. Apparently in the prayers that evening the vicar had thanked God 'for the succour that has recently come to this parish'.

\*       \*       \*

Vicar: I felt I had them on the edge of their seats tonight dear.
Wife: So did I. They were trying to muster the nerve to get up and go home.

\*       \*       \*

A man met his daughter at Heathrow Airport after her holiday in Nairobi. To his surprise, she got off the plane with a very striking-looking man. He wore a fancy headdress of ostrich feathers and a leopard-skin loincloth. In one hand was a shield and in the other a spear. A piece of bone went through his nose and his necklace was made of animal teeth. The father was even more surprised when his daughter introduced him as her new husband.

'You silly stupid girl,' he said, 'why do you never listen properly. Your mother and I simply said we hoped you would marry a *rich* doctor.'

*     *     *

A little boy is showing his school friend the wedding picture of his parents that stood on the piano in the sitting room. He says, 'And that's when daddy got mummy to come and work for us.'

*     *     *

The normal baptism by immersion was taking place in the local Baptist church. The minister explained, 'There is nothing magical about this water. It is exactly the same water that we shall use later to make the tea and coffee.'

*     *     *

The report in the local paper on the Remembrance Day service was somewhat marred by the misprint that appeared in the last sentence, which declared, 'And finally the congregation stood in silence as the Last Post was sounded from the gallery by a lone burglar.'

*     *     *

Backhanded compliments that often come the way of the clergy:

'I don't care what people say about your sermons, vicar, I quite like them.'

'I have to hand it to you, vicar, you always find something to fill up the time.'

'If I had known you were going to preach a good sermon like that, vicar, I would have brought a friend. She's been wanting to come for ages.'

\* \* \*

The vicar was anxious to improve the morals of the young men in his county parish, and took every opportunity to get his message across. One late evening, whilst taking his dog for a walk, he met a young man carrying a lantern, and he asked him what he was doing. 'I be lookin' for a nice lass so that I can do a bit o' courting,' he was told.

'When I was your age,' said the vicar, 'I didn't go looking for a girl with a lighted lantern.'

'Well vicar, all I can say,' replied the yokel, 'is when I looks at your missus, might 'ave been better if you 'ad.'

\* \* \*

A man acquired a girlfriend who is a medium in the local spiritualist church. He eventually proposes marriage in a rather novel way. Down on one knee he pops the question with, 'Alice, will I marry you?'

\* \* \*

There's nothing like a little exercise to change a man's life – especially if it's a walk down the aisle.

\* \* \*

One Sunday morning little Johnny was being sent to church as usual and his father gave him two coins – a pound and a 50p piece. 'Put which you think best in the collection,' he was told.

When he arrived home his father questioned him regarding which coin he had put on the plate in church.

'I wanted to do the Christian thing, dad,' he said, 'and at first I thought I ought to give the pound, but then I remembered it says in the Bible, "The Lord loveth a cheerful giver", and I jolly well knew I'd be a lot more cheerful if I gave the 50p and spent the pound on toffees. So that's what I did.'

\* \* \*

The preacher was getting steamed up. 'What are you heading for,' he thundered, 'heaven or hell ... which is it to be ... bliss or blisters?'

\* \* \*

The organist was so bad, the sidesman at the back used to have a competition with the introduction to every hymn. They copied the idea from a TV quiz show call *Name that tune in ten.*

\* \* \*

The woman was quite excited as she dashed up to the bishop in the back of the church after the service to thank him for his address. 'Oh bishop,' she enthused, 'what a sermon, what a sermon! Every word was superfluous!' Then gathering her breath she declared, 'It ought to be published post ... posthumously.'

\* \* \*

It is fairly well known that the present pope, John Paul 11, was as a young man a keen football player in his native Poland. He was apparently a gifted goalkeeper. However, it is said on good authority that he would never have made it into the national team for he had one great weakness – he couldn't handle the crosses.

\* \* \*

Advice to preachers from the great Baptist preacher, Charles Spurgeon (mid 1800s), 'When you speak of heaven, let your face light up: when you speak of hell, your ordinary, everyday faces will do!' He also said, 'Some preachers would make good martyrs. They are so dry they would burn well.'

\* \* \*

Husband: I was so proud when I heard you describe me to your friend as a model husband.
Wife: Don't get too carried away, for you do appreciate, I hope, that a model is but a small replica of the real thing.

\* \* \*

Robert Runcie (Archbishop of Canterbury 1980-91) said that some folk seem to misinterpret the well-known words used in the Communion Service, 'Drink ye all of this', and are obviously of the opinion that this is an invitation to drain the chalice.

\* \* \*

An Irishman was making an application to join the army. The recruiting sergeant was taking down the details. The applicant gave his full name, Patrick O'Lord O'Grady. The Sergeant was curious: 'Was your middle name given because your parents were very religious?' he asked
    'No sir, it was because as the parson was baptising me he dropped me in the font.'

\* \* \*

The vicar preached a dazzling sermon that everyone admired. The curate was particularly impressed and offered his congratulations after the service. However, the following week at the staff meeting he had a further comment. 'What rascals these American theologians are,' he said, 'for I have just discovered that they have stolen that wonderful sermon of yours and published it – 10 years ago!'

\* \* \*

Bishop Victor Whitsey of Chester (1974-81) was about to give the blessing at the end of the service at a church in Northwich. A small boy of about five years of age had followed him into the sanctuary by crawling through the altar rails, and at this point began to howl. The bishop in his kindly way picked him up in his arms and said, 'There, there, what's the matter son?'

In the loudest possible voice, the little lad bellowed, 'I've bumped mi bloody head, that's what's up.'

\* \* \*

Parishioner: 'The most misleading thing about our vicar is that he brings his sermons to church in a *brief*case!'

\* \* \*

My wife and I had to get divorced because of an illness: we were sick of each other!

\* \* \*

A woman called at the music shop to enquire yet again whether her order for Handel's Oratorio was available. Once again she was disappointed, and complained, 'This is disgraceful, I've been waiting more than six weeks for the *Messiah*.'

The proprietor, Mr Joshua Rosenburg apologised, but then shrugged his shoulders in a gesture of resignation and said, 'You vait for the Messiah for six veeks, six veeks, and you think that is something to complain of?'

\* \* \*

The vicar had just preached about the rich giving to the poor. Afterwards the churchwarden congratulated him on a powerful sermon. 'It was at least 50% successful, vicar,' he said, 'I think you convinced the poor.'

\*     \*     \*

Judge passing sentence on bigamist: 'I must now send you to prison, for this is one time in life when, in fact, two rites do make a wrong.'

\*     \*     \*

The old verger was telling a visitor about the services in the parish church. 'And the vicar's sermons,' he said, 'are what I call ox-head sermons.'

'I suppose you mean they are powerful and forward-looking?' suggested the visitor.

'No, not that,' came the reply, 'I mean he has two good points and a lot of bull in between.'

\*     \*     \*

Vicar giving the notices: 'This being Easter Sunday, we will ask Mrs Lewis to come forward and lay an egg on the altar.'

\*     \*     \*

A woman tells how one Sunday morning in church an elderly gentleman collapsed in his seat. She says, 'Being in the St John's Ambulance Brigade, I went to him and advised him to keep his head down so that the blood could flow to the brain. To assist him in this, I gently pushed his head further down between his knees. After a minute or so he seemed to recover and pushed his way up breathing hard and with a very red face. He spluttered, "Madam, do you do this to everybody who happens to drop a hymn book?"'

\*     \*     \*

Trying to get something across to a congregation by preaching, is like trying to fill a long-necked bottle by throwing water over it!

\*     \*     \*

First parishioner: Excuse me sir, but you are occupewing my pie.

Second parishioner: I am so sorry. But the churchwarden sewed me into this sheet.

*     *     *

The couple were in the vestry signing the marriage registers, but the bridegroom found that the ballpoint pen would not write. The vicar said, 'Just put your weight on it.' It was only afterwards that he saw that the man had managed to write his name with it, but had then added, 'about 11 and a half stone'.

*     *     *

Advice to would-be preachers at a theological college from one of the more experienced teachers:

The Lord's Prayer has 56 words.

The Apostles' Creed has 109.

The Ten Commandments has 297.

An EEC directive on the import of caramel has 26,911.

The students were left to draw their own conclusions!

*     *     *

A story vouched for by the organist who was present concerns a spring wedding when tax incentives made that time of the year particularly popular. In a Lancashire church there were no fewer than nine weddings booked for the same Saturday, most of which were to be taken by the vicar, though during his lunch break, the newly priested curate was to officiate at two. All went well in spite of the nervousness of the curate, and the vicar resumed control with the 2 o'clock ceremony. The service followed the normal pattern, and soon the vows were being taken. 'I George take thee Margaret to my wedded wife, to have and to hold ...'

Then it was the bride's turn, 'Say after me, I Margaret take thee George to my wedded husband.'

Silence.

The vicar tried again, but once more there was no response.

'Say the words,' pleaded the vicar.

'Not likely,' said the bride, 'why should I. I'm not Margaret.'

At this stage George joined in rather belatedly with, 'No, and for't record, I'm not George neither.'

The vicar turned despairingly to the organist with the plea, 'Play something', as he led the couple to the vestry to sort out the problem. At this very time, the real George and Margaret were outside having their photographs taken. They had appeared before the curate an hour earlier. He had forgotten to remove the top sheet of the pad with the names on it, which was inside the clergy prayer book.

\*     \*     \*

Have you ever noticed how small a pound can look in the supermarket, yet so big in the church!

\*     \*     \*

Parishioner to departing vicar: I am so sorry you are leaving us, your sermons to me have been like water to a drowning man.'

\*     \*     \*

This is said to be a true story of a vicar who disliked fancy or topical names being requested for babies whom he was to baptise. He had even been known to quibble at *Hazel*, saying, 'You have all those lovely Biblical names to chose from, and you want to call her after a nut?' However, he was caught out in 1969 when the parents indicated that they wanted their child called Buzz. 'I suppose you are calling him after the astronaut Buzz Aldrin aren't you, just because he happens to have walked on the moon. That's a very silly thing to do, for the name will date the boy and make him a laughing stock when the astronaut is long forgotten.'

The parents knew the Bible better than the vicar and referred him to Abraham's nephew who bore that name (Genesis 22: 21). And for good measure they threw in 1 Chronicles 5: 14 and Jeremiah 25: 23.

*　　*　　*

A correspondent to a newspaper wrote, 'Our well-built, six-foot-tall curate read out his own marriage banns, and finished by saying, "If anyone knows just cause or impediment why we should not be joined together in holy matrimony, let him meet me outside the south door at the end of the service".'

*　　*　　*

The vicar was highly delighted when he was told that sermons brought home to people the love and mercy of God. That is, until he was reminded that the Bible says, 'The love of God passeth all understanding, and his mercy endureth for ever.'

*　　*　　*

Bigamy is having one wife too many: monogamy means much the same kind of thing.

*　　*　　*

The old bishop had been unfairly attacked in the newspapers several times, and felt he had the opportunity to get his own back when the ladies and gentleman of Fleet Street attended a special service for the media in the cathedral. He diligently searched the scriptures for a suitable text for his sermon, and it was with some satisfaction that when the day came he was able to announce it from the pulpit: he had chosen Luke 19: 3 – 'And he sought to see Jesus, but could not for the press.'

*　　*　　*

44

My husband and I were very happy for about 25 years – and then we met!

*      *      *

Inexperienced curate beginning his sermon: 'The Bible tells us to "Come apart" and I hope you will all come apart this evening.'

*      *      *

As Henry VIII said to his wife, 'Don't worry, I won't keep you long.'

*      *      *

One sensible vicar had a prayer written inside the pulpit as a constant reminder. It said:
> Lord, fill my mouth with worthwhile stuff
> And nudge me when they've had enough

*      *      *

When the Church Council complained that the vicar was introducing some high church practices, he came out with a piece of sound pastoral advice: 'Remember,' he said, 'as far as I'm concerned, it's not the boy that's holding the candle, it's the candle that's holding the boy.'

*      *      *

They say he loves watching a video of his wedding, though apparently he always plays it backwards. Says he loves to see himself leaving the church a free man!

*      *      *

The churchwardens were comparing the performances in the pulpit of vicar and curate. 'I much prefer the curate myself,' said one. The other asked him why.

'Well,' he replied, 'the curate says "in conclusion" and then concludes. The vicar says, "lastly" and then lasts and lasts.'

\*     \*     \*

Notice outside church: NO PARKING – THIS MEANS THOU!

\*     \*     \*

# Chapter Three

## PARISH LIFE

### (All Craters Great and Small)

The vicar returned from his afternoon visiting to find a tramp on his hands and knees on the vicarage lawn. Somewhat surprised he asked him what he was doing. 'I'm so hungry, sir, I'm eating the grass.'

'You poor, poor fellow,' exclaimed the vicar, 'follow me.' He led him through the side gate to the back of the house. 'There,' he said pointing to the back lawn, 'you can eat there, the grass is longer.'

\*     \*     \*

Notice board: WHY PRAY WHEN YOU CAN WORRY AND TAKE PILLS?

\*     \*     \*

Question: Which is the odd one out – *The Church Times*, *The Catholic Herald*, *The Universe*, The Queen Mother?
Answer: The Queen Mother, for she is the one with the good circulation.

\*     \*     \*

Old Jock, the local drunk in a Scottish village, had fallen down some steps on his way home from the pub and lay critically ill. The minister, who was known to enjoy a dram or two himself, was summoned to the bedside. He knelt down and prayed.

'Closer, closer,' urged Jock. Then, 'Say them again,' he pleaded when the minister had done. The minister complied, only to be asked again. 'Once more mon, once more.'

'I didna' think ye were all that fond o' prayer,' said the minister finally.

'It's no the prayers ah want,' said Jock, 'it's yer breath.'

\* \* \*

The new vicar was aware that people were laughing at him behind his back – he spotted the sniggers several times. Eventually the churchwarden explained that unfortunately the village postman was also the village gossip, and that this same man had recently delivered a postcard to the vicar from a woman in his previous parish. She had written to say that his successor had arrived at the church he had recently left and that he seemed a very nice man. She had concluded with, 'His sermons are not bad, but he doesn't hold me the way you used to.'

\* \* \*

The vicar reported to the church meeting that his efforts to change the address of the old folks' home in the parish had met with success. He had managed to persuade the town council that St Peter's Avenue was to be preferred to the more ominous St Peter's Close.

\* \* \*

The scene is the Royal Mint. A friendship has been struck up between a newly minted pound and an equally new penny. They were very sorry when the time came for them to part and to be sent out into the world as coinage of the realm. The years went by, and then one day to their surprise they found themselves in the same purse. They were delighted and began to exchange their experiences. The pound boasted of the great life he had had, describing how he had been on Concorde, how he had been in the pocket of a duke, and that he had even attended a garden party at Buckingham Palace. 'Now, what about you?' he asked.

The penny modestly admitted that nothing very special had happened to him. 'I seem to have been mainly in children's purses,' he said, 'and in the till of sweet shops: been on the buses many a time, but nothing out of the ordinary.'

The pound was very condescending, 'Oh you poor thing, what a shame, such a dull life.'

The penny was quick to retaliate. 'Please don't feel sorry for me.' He said, 'for at least I have a better chance of getting to heaven than you.'

The pound enquired how this could possibly be.

'Well,' replied the penny, 'at least I've been to church practically every Sunday for the past 20 years.'

*     *     *

'I have noticed again and again since I have been in the church, that lay interest in ecclesiastical matters is often the prelude to insanity.' (Evelyn Waugh 1903-66)

*     *     *

It often fell to the lot of the Bishop of Birkenhead in the 1980s to take a short service of blessing at the launching ceremony of a new ship built at Cammel Laird's. There were always lots of VIPs present, of course, and it was also customary to invite groups of children from the schools in the area. After one such occasion, the children in a particular school were given the task of writing an essay on what they had seen. A little girl gave a vivid description of the event, and concluded with, 'And after the bishop had said the prayers, he told us all to stand up straight, and then we sang the National Curriculum.'

*     *     *

The vicar knew that Charlie, one of his parishioners, was a bit 'thick'. Even that was putting it mildly! The man worked at a sawmill and, alas, one day a great plank fell off a stack and hit him on the head. He was rushed to hospital and as soon as the vicar heard of the event he went to see him. The priest was relieved to see him sitting up in bed smiling with no apparent sign of an injury apart from a bandaged foot. Somewhat puzzled the vicar said, 'But I was given to understand the plank fell on your head, Charlie.'

'Quite true,' came the reply, 'but you have to remember I was standing on a nail at the time.'

\* \* \*

There was just one candidate for the verger's job and in many ways he appeared very suitable. The only problem was that the man had the reputation of being a heavy drinker. The vicar and churchwardens decided on a subtle psychological ploy to discover whether or not this was true. The man was told to say the first thing that came into his head when a word or phrase was put to him. One warden began, snapping out the words, 'Bells and Teachers.'

Without hesitation the man replied, 'A noble sound, and a noble profession.'

The second warden tried his luck: 'Grants and Haigs,' he cried.

Again there was a quick response: 'Two great generals, one American, one British.'

It was the vicar's turn now. He thought his colleagues had made it a bit too easy. 'OK,' he said, 'what about Tetley's and VAT 69?'

Quick as a flash came the answer, 'Ah yes, those lovely teabags, and would that be the pope's telephone number?'

\* \* \*

In a pastoral report on the city centre, it was sadly announced that several churches would have to close due to 'swindling congregations'.

\* \* \*

The vicar was a notoriously bad driver and narrowly missed hitting the postman on the vicarage drive. He stopped and apologised. The postman claimed that in diving for cover he had damaged a leg and might want to claim compensation. The vicar gave him a visiting card so that he could get in touch with him later if he wished. However, as the clergyman sped away, the man's anger was increased as he read the message on the card, for it said, 'The Reverend John Browne is very sorry to have missed you, but hopes to make contact with you soon'.

\*     \*     \*

Britain owes its greatness to the four great races found within its shores, namely the Derby, the Grand National, the Cheltenham Gold Cup and the Oaks. The actual inhabitants of the islands are a mixed bunch but have one thing in common – they are fond of religious exercises. For example:

- The Scots are famous for keeping the Sabbath, and anything else they can lay their hands on.
- The Welsh pray on their knees and on their neighbours.
- The Irish do not know what they want but are prepared to die for it.
- The English are a race of self-made men, there by relieving the Almighty of a dreadful responsibility.

\*     \*     \*

Biblical advice on how to vote from Ecclesiastes 10: 2 – 'A wise man's heart inclines him towards the right, but a fool's heart towards the left.'

\*     \*     \*

He stayed at such a sleazy hotel, that to get a Gideon Bible you had to ring room service.

\*     \*     \*

From a parish magazine in Devonshire comes this fascinating item: 'The voluntary work in the churchyard was completed by the resurfacing of the path when, to the applause of all who had helped, the vicar and his wife rolled in the new gravel.'

\* \* \*

The priest was speeding along a country road in Ireland when he ran over a hare. He ground to a halt and, accompanied by his passenger, walked over to the prostrate animal lying senseless by the side of the road.

'Oh father, you've killed the poor thing,' cried the passenger accusingly. But the priest wasn't listening. He was back at the car extracting a small bottle from his briefcase. He returned to the animal, took out the cork, and carefully sprinkled a few drops of a colourless liquid over the lifeless creature. Immediately there were slight movements of the legs. A few more drops were sprinkled and the movements increased, until it got to its feet, shook itself and bounded off into the adjacent field.

'Oh father, a miracle, a miracle, a veritable miracle,' exclaimed the excited passenger, 'did you use holy water?'

'Of course not,' replied the priest, 'just ordinary hair restorer!'

\* \* \*

An old priest vouches for the truth of the following conversation, which took place in the street:

Lady: 'Morning vicar, sorry I haven't been able to get to church for the last two or three weeks, but my daughter-in-law has had to go into hospital and now the bitch has had pups.'

From the same source comes the story of an embarrassing moment in a maternity ward where he was visiting the mother of newly born twins.

Vicar: 'Well congratulations, my dear, how splendid.

What lovely babies. But they are very much alike. Now, believe me, that's going to be a big problem for you, I'm afraid. How on earth are you going to tell them apart?'

Mother: 'I think even I can manage that vicar, one's a boy and the other's a girl.'

\*     \*     \*

Church notice board:

### ST THOMAS' CHURCH
### THE MESSIAH HERE
### NEXT SUNDAY

\*     \*     \*

'As far as I can see,' said a man talking to his Jewish friend, 'the only difference between us is that you don't go to the synagogue on a Saturday and I don't go to church on a Sunday.'

\*     \*     \*

An old lady tells of an experience of many years ago when she returned home after being in London for several weeks. On the first Sunday back, she was in her usual place in the parish church. At the end of the service she made her way out past the vicar who was engaged in conversation with a group of ladies.

She writes: I was endeavouring to slip by him when he suddenly grasped me by the coat collar and hauled me back in reverse. In front of the others he bellowed, 'Where the devil have you been?'

I couldn't believe my ears, so asked rather archly, 'What was that father?' He repeated the question in an even louder voice. I looked at him as at a bug through a microscope and replied, 'May I respectfully point out to you father, that when the Prodigal Son returned home his father went out to meet him and said how good it was to have him home again. He didn't say, "Where the devil have you been?"'

The vicar looked at me in utter disbelief and then roared, 'Get out!'

I didn't look back until I had reached the corner of the street. When I did, I could see the priest was waving his biretta over his head in a circular motion and howling with mirth.

*       *       *

The vicar gave out copies of his annual report, and then implored the members of the church council to 'take it home, read, mark, learn and inwardly digest it, and if any part of it causes distress or unease, please bring it up at our next meeting'.

*       *       *

After the 'Night of the Long Knives' when Harold Macmillan sacked half his cabinet in order to bolster his failing government, he was attacked in the House of Commons by Harold Wilson, who said that he couldn't do better than let the Bible describe what the prime minister had done. He said, 'Surely this is a classic example of "Greater love hath no man than this, that a man lay down his friends for his life".'

*       *       *

It was said that although Birkenhead had its rough and difficult areas, there was no disputing the fact that its citizens had been environmentally conscious for years, and in fact lead-free churches had long been the norm!

*       *       *

Church notice board: DON'T LET WORRY KILL YOU – LET THE CHURCH HELP

*       *       *

One Sunday in Belfast three Protestant ladies went to the local Roman Catholic Church as a gesture of goodwill. They arrived a few minutes late, the service had just started and the church was full. The priest knew them by sight and wanted them to feel welcome. He whispered to the server, 'Quick, three chairs for the Protestant ladies.'

At once the server leapt to his feet, flung both hands up into the air, and cried, 'Three cheers for the Protestant ladies, hip, hip hooray ...'

There was a marvellous response from the congregation and the roof was nearly lifted off. Normal service was then resumed.

\*     \*     \*

Chairman at a convention of charismatics: 'Those in favour of the motion, hands down please.'

\*     \*     \*

A parson and two sailors were the only occupants of the railway carriage, and in a loud voice the sailors talked about their plans for the next few days while they were on leave. 'I'm going to get drunk every night,' boasted one, 'what about you?'

The other said he had other plans – 'It's girls, girls, girls for me.'

Silence descended for a while as they produced newspapers and settled into them. After a while one of them addressed the parson. 'Excuse me, sir,' he began, 'but I wonder if you can help: I'm reading here about sciatica and I wonder if you can tell me what it is?'

The parson saw his opportunity. 'Yes indeed I can,' he replied, 'sciatica is a very unpleasant pain in the back, often caused by strong drink and leading an immoral life.'

'Thank you for telling me,' said the sailor, 'I'm just reading here that the Bishop of London is suffering from it.'

*      *      *

A favourite Jewish story tells how one day an old rabbi was out walking with his grandson. They came across a blind man begging by the side of the road. 'Here,' said the rabbi, 'go and put this coin in his box.' The little boy did as he was told. When he got back his grandfather reprimanded him. 'You should have raised your hat to him as a sign of respect,' he was told.

'But he's blind,' protested the boy, 'he couldn't have seen it anyway.

'You should still have done,' said the old man, 'he might have been an impostor.'

*      *      *

There was a strict rule of silence in the monastery, but once every five years one monk was allowed to speak. When it was Brother Bernard's turn he stood up in the refectory and said, 'The porridge is disgusting'.

Five years went by and this time it was Brother Joseph's turn. He got up and said, 'The porridge is lovely.'

It was Brother Francis who was first on his feet five years later. 'I'm leaving the monastery,' he announced, 'I can't stand all this bickering about the porridge.'

*      *      *

An Anglo-Catholic church in London made an intriguing promise in its monthly newsletter: 'Hot smacks are available after High Mass on Wednesdays in the crypt.'

*      *      *

Some people maintain that there is a direct correlation between racism and stupidity, and the following incident seems to verify this.

'I'd send them all back, blacks, browns, yellows, the lot – Turks, Bosnians, Asians, I'd get rid of the lot of 'em,' fulminated the chap in the pub.

'Hold on,' protested the vicar who happened to be there, 'before you know it you could be talking about euthanasia.'

'Exactly, and I'd send those ruddy Euthanasians back as well.'

*     *     *

Church notice board: The Prayers for Peace have been cancelled this month owing to the arrival of the new vicar.

*     *     *

Three missionaries were captured by a tribe of cannibals; they were tied to adjacent trees in front of the large cooking pots that already had fires burning beneath them. The cannibals were busy preparing the vegetables when the first missionary asked one of them, 'What is your favourite food?' The cannibal replied, 'Beans.' Encouraged by this, the second missionary asked another cannibal the same question. Again came the reply, 'Beans.'

'I think we're in luck's way,' whispered the third missionary, 'they are obviously vegetarians, probably doing all this to frighten us.' With increasing confidence he addressed the leader of the tribe. 'You all seem to like eating beans, is that right?'

'Sure is,' said the chief licking his lips, 'there's nothing we like more than human beings.'

*     *     *

Miss Jones made a great fuss of the man at the bus stop. 'What a pleasure it is to see you,' she gushed, 'how lovely to bump into you like this.' It was at this point she realised she had mistaken him for someone else. She had thought he was connected with her Sunday school work, and now covered with confusion and blushing with embarrassment she stammered, 'Oh err ... so sorry, do forgive me, but I thought you were the father of one of my children.'

*     *     *

There was a very fat nun who dearly loved her food. She was cautioned by the Mother Superior on the subject of greed. 'Remember,' she was told, 'the Bible says that we are temples of the Holy Spirit, and therefore we should respect our bodies and show restraint.'

For a while the lesson apparently went home and it was noticed that the nun ate much less than before. But then, alas, it became obvious at meal times that she was back to her former ways. Again she was on the carpet for a reprimand. 'You seem to be forgetting what I said about being temples of the Holy Spirit sister,' said her Superior.

With a beatific smile the nun replied, 'Well, it was while I was praying the other day Mother, that I seemed to hear a voice that said, 'Sister, you are not a temple of the Holy Spirit, you are a basilica.'

\*     \*     \*

There was a very good attendance for the church meeting and the vicar wondered whether the misprint on the agenda was responsible. It was the first item that might have attracted some. It said, 'The meeting will be gin with prayer'.

\*     \*     \*

Two old sweats were sharing a shell-hole on the Somme in 1917. The shells were whistling over thick and fast. 'I'm scared stiff,' said Bill, 'know any prayers, Charlie?'

'Prayers!' said his mate, 'what do you think this is, a Sunday school outing?' The shells seemed to get even closer and louder. Bill tried again. 'Know any hymns, Charlie?'

'Hymns! What do you think I am, a flippin' choirboy?'

Time passed, and soon a shell exploded on the very edge of the hole making them think their number was well and truly up. Bill whipped off his tin helmet, held it out to his companion and pleaded, 'Well, we must do something religious, let's have a collection.'

\*     \*     \*

There was keen rivalry between two curates for the job of vicar in a highly desirable suburban parish that had just become vacant. One of them, Jones, talked about it with his vicar and wondered whether sending the bishop a couple of bottles of Champagne might help him secure the appointment. The vicar was horrified and advised strongly against it, adding that in his opinion the other priest, Robinson, was slightly senior and would probably be appointed anyway. However, he turned out to be wrong, and a short time afterwards Jones got the job. He was highly delighted and told his vicar, 'I think it was the Champagne that did the trick, two bottles of the best bubbly, a bit pricey but worth every penny.'

The vicar was aghast: 'Don't tell me you actually sent it?' he said.

'Oh yes,' replied Jones, 'but of course I sent it in Robinson's name.'

\* \* \*

Our vicar has such a low profile in the parish that many of us think he should have been a limbo dancer.

\* \* \*

Winston Churchill was being interviewed as prospective candidate for a parliamentary seat in the north of England.

Chairman: 'Would you describe yourself as a pillar of the church?'

Churchill: 'No sir, not a pillar, more a flying buttress, for I support the church from the outside.'

\* \* \*

The famous Canon Spooner (1844-1930) not only got his words mixed up as everybody knows, but was genuinely woolly minded, particularly in old age. A well-authenticated story tells how one day in an Oxford street he met an undergraduate and invited him to supper in his rooms. He said, 'My dear chap you really must come, Thompson's coming.'

A little embarrassed the man replied, 'But sir, *I am* Thompson.'

'Oh dear, how very stupid of me,' said the canon, 'of course you are, of course you are, but do come all the same, I think you'll like him.'

\* \* \*

Our curate is so narrow minded I can sometimes see his ears rubbing together!

\* \* \*

A Scottish minister called to see a poorly parishioner. Before taking him into the sick room, the woman told him that her husband was seriously ill and his mind was wandering. They entered, and the wife went over to the bed and told the sick man that he had a visitor. 'It's the minister,' she said, 'I know you'll be glad to see him.'

'Och aye,' he mumbled, 'o' course I'm glad, he's a fine man and a splendid preacher.'

The woman turned to the minister. 'There you are,' she said, 'I did warn you he was rambling.'

\* \* \*

There was once an Irish monk who had a disagreement with the abbot and other senior members of the monastery. They summoned him to a meeting of the chapter, the body that ran the place. They were furious when he didn't turn up, and even angrier when they read the reason why. His letter simply said, 'Sorry I cannot be present at the meeting today.' He signed himself, 'The Holy Spirit'.

\* \* \*

The vicar always claimed that he never mixed politics and religion, and that no one in the parish even knew how he voted. There were some in the parish who thought otherwise, claiming that it was only necessary to note the choice of hymns that followed an election. If the Conservatives got in, they invariably found themselves singing *Now thank we all our God*. If Labour had triumphed it was always *Oh God our help in ages past, our hope for years to come*. If the Liberal Democrats did well they sang *God moves in a mysterious way His wonders to perform*.

\* \* \*

'Oh Lord,' cried the lay reader, getting very worked up in the prayers, 'send your richest blessings on this congregation, and give them all clean hearts, give them pure hearts, give them sweet hearts.'

\* \* \*

Church notice board: UNLIKE THE POST OFFICE, WE HAVE TWO COLLECTIONS EVERY SUNDAY

\* \* \*

A true story comes from Wales. Many years ago a beggar stood on the bridge in Carmarthen plying his trade. He held out his cap to every passer-by and with eloquent body language pleaded for a contribution. Around his neck was a piece of string supporting a notice on his chest, which in large letters described the man's predicament. It said, 'Blinded in a colliery explosion'. A priest happened to be crossing the bridge at the time and he challenged the man. 'You can obviously see,' he said, 'it seems to me that you are an impostor.'

The man became very agitated, and replied, 'Well I might be able to see, but I can't read, tell me what my board says.' It was read to him.

'Oh Lord,' said the beggar, 'it's a mistake, I've picked up the wrong one, I was supposed to have "Deaf and Dumb".'

\* \* \*

Church notice board: PRAY, DO NOT PARK HERE!

\* \* \*

A Freudian slip from a church newsletter in Cornwall: 'Some of our friends who made regular contributions to the church have died during the year, but we would like to think there are others who would consider doing the same. Names can be handed to the vicar.'

\* \* \*

Sister Martha ran out of the doctor's consulting room screaming her head off. The next patient to go in was naturally curious. 'The sister was in a terrible state,' she said, 'have you just given her some bad news?'

'As a matter of fact,' said the doctor, 'I have just told her she's pregnant.'

'Oh surely not, not Sister Martha!'

'No, no, not really,' chuckled the doctor, 'but I have just cured her hiccups.'

\* \* \*

Caller: 'Hello, hello, is that the vicar? Good: I have to tell you that my little girl has just swallowed a 20p piece.'
Vicar: 'But why are you telling this to me?'
Caller: 'My wife says you can get money out of anybody.'

\* \* \*

The new curate of a rural parish thought he ought to familiarise himself with country ways and decided to make a start by teaching himself how to milk a cow. Armed with a pail and a three-legged stool, he managed to corner a poor cow in the meadow and after one or two stumbles and falls eventually got going. The cow soon realised that here was an amateur, not to be trusted, and moved off a few yards. The curate lifted his pail and stool, followed her and began milking again. It wasn't long before exactly the same thing happened, and once more the curate had to shift his position. It was at this moment that the local farmer arrived on the scene and with obvious surprise and annoyance cried out, 'And what do you think you're doing?'

The rather flustered curate replied, 'About three miles to the gallon, I think.'

\* \* \*

Kitchen notice in church hall: Ladies, when you have emptied the teapots, please stand upside down in the sink

\* \* \*

Albert staggers out of the pub and collides with a nun in the street. She raises a reproving finger and lectures him on the evils of drink. 'Wasting your money and ruining your health with alcohol,' she says.

He defends himself vigorously. 'A little social drinking never did anybody any harm, and it actually does a person good, makes him feel better. Bet you've never tried it, you're condemning something you know nothing about.' Warming to this theme he continues, 'Look, let me get you a glass of whisky, and then give me your honest opinion as to whether it warms you up and gives you a bit of a lift.'

At first the nun refuses, but eventually she agrees on one condition, that the whisky be served in a teacup, 'for what would people think if they saw a nun drinking whisky in the street.'

Albert returns to the bar and orders a double whisky, 'but would you mind please serving it in a teacup.'

'Oh gosh,' says the barman as he picks up a cup from under the bar, 'so she's back, is she, Sister Martha, the alcoholic nun!'

*     *     *

How do you rate your new curate?' the vicar was asked by a colleague.

'Well, let me put it this way,' came the reply, 'if you were a football manager I could honestly say that five million wouldn't buy him – and I'm one of them!'

*     *     *

The vicar did seem to spend a lot of time cutting the grass in the churchyard, never less than three whole days a week. When he was criticised for this at a church council meeting he silenced his critics by explaining, 'Since about half of my salary comes from the dead, it seems only right that they should have about half of my time.'

*     *     *

Poor old Reuben was set upon by a thug as came out of the synagogue one Saturday morning. The final blow to the chin was accompanied by the taunt, 'And that's for sinking the *Titanic*.'

Even in his weakened state, Reuben couldn't let that pass unchallenged. 'What do you mean?' he cried, 'the *Titanic* was sunk by an iceberg.'

The assailant grabbed him by the scruff of the neck, and with his face only inches away, shouted, 'Iceberg, Goldberg, Lindbergh, Rosenburg, what's it matter, you're all flippin' related.'

*     *     *

The parish had more than its share of bossy, awkward folk and as a consequence there was a rapid turnover of vicars. When the latest one arrived, the churchwarden talked to him about the outside notice board, and there was something of a threat in the suggestion he made: 'Do you mind if we just put your name on it in chalk?' But he got as good as he gave from the young priest, who replied, 'Sure, that's OK provided you also fasten a sponge to it on a piece of string.'

\*       \*       \*

Church notice board: The ladies of the parish have cast off clothing of every kind. They can be seen in the basement on Saturday mornings.

\*       \*       \*

When the vicar discovered his house was overrun with mice, a kindly parishioner presented him with a kitten, which in time she hoped would solve the problem. 'She's only small now, but in a few weeks she'll be a real hunter, I can tell,' said the woman. The vicar was truly grateful, and after a few weeks took the cat to the vet to be sterilised for he did not want the bother of kittens. The vet quickly decided there was no need to worry, for in fact the cat was a tom. That solved another problem too, for there had been a dispute over the cat's name: now it was unanimously agreed that he should be called Danny – after Danny La Rue of course!

\*       \*       \*

The train was travelling at full speed through the Irish countryside when there was an important announcement over the intercom. 'Emergency, emergency,' boomed the loud speaker, 'is there a Catholic priest on board?' It was obvious after a few minutes that the appeal had been unsuccessful, for soon came another announcement, 'Please, please, this is urgent, is there an Anglican vicar on board?' That too met with no response, for before long came a third frantic appeal, 'Is there a Jewish rabbi among the passengers?' Again there was no response.

It was at this juncture that a small timid-looking man came forward to the guard and said, 'Excuse me, but I'm a Methodist minister, could I be of assistance?'

'No sorr, no sorr, I think not,' replied the guard, for sure it's a corkscrew we're after.'

\*     \*     \*

From a parish magazine in London: Thursday at 6.30pm, aerobics followed by a talk on sex in the church hall.

\*     \*     \*

The parish faced an urgent problem – there really were bats in the belfry. The vicar and churchwardens discussed the problem at length. One warden was sure he could solve the problem. 'Leave it to me,' he said, and soon he was back with a large net. The other two watched from below as he skilfully cast the net around the belfry and captured every single bat. Soon the whole lot were in the back of his van as he sped off to the nearby moors to release the bats as far from the church as possible. Alas, it was all in vain, for the bats were back in the belfry before he had completed the return journey.

At this stage the other warden took over. 'I'm sick of all this pussyfooting,' he grumbled, 'this is the way to solve the problem.' He produced a double-barrelled shotgun and proceeded to blast away upwards. The bats' radar system worked perfectly and they were all out before any casualties were suffered, and all back the minute the shooting stopped, more visible than ever because of the shafts of sunlight that now shone through the many holes in the church roof.

The vicar was furious at the damage, but then into his mind came a brilliant idea that he knew would solve the problem once and for all. 'Got it!' he cried, 'I know exactly what to do; all I need now is a bowl of water. Then I will go into the belfry and baptise every single bat: tomorrow I will get the bishop to come and confirm them, and believe me, after that they will fly away and be seen no more.'

\*     \*     \*

Canon Bill Vanstone (1923-1999) was a wonderful parish priest and outstanding theologian. He used to tell the story of a Mrs S, an elderly widow who lived near his vicarage when he was incumbent of a large housing estate in Lancashire. Although this lady had some admirable qualities, it did seem she was genetically incapable of admitting that anything was *good* or *nice*. If you said it was a nice day, she would insist there was quite a cold breeze: or if you passed the opinion that the family next door seemed rather pleasant, she would shake her head and mutter that you didn't know as much about them as she did. Bill decided to try to get her to cross this barrier, and one Sunday got his housekeeper to make an extra helping of a particularly nice lunch. He had told Mrs S that he would take her midday meal round for her, which he did. Later that day, he called to pick up the 'empties'. They were ready for him, washed and wrapped. 'Thank you vicar,' she said.

Bill pressed for an opinion: 'But did you enjoy it?' he enquired, hoping that at last she would be complimentary about something.

She put on her sad expression, and said, 'Ah vicar, if only I could have tasted it.'

\*　　\*　　\*

A report on the annual meeting in the parish magazine said, 'Mr Johnson has accepted the office of churchwarden. We could not get a better man.'

\*　　\*　　\*

It was customary at one time for the collections on Easter day to be given to the incumbent, and this came in handy on one occasion when several boys in a playground were boasting about the amount of money earned by their fathers. One said his father was a surgeon and charged a thousand pounds for an operation. Another declared that his father was a lawyer and got two thousand pounds for defending someone in court. They turned to the third boy and in a very superior way asked, 'Well, what about your father?'

He was hard-pressed to try to match their boasting, but finally came up with, 'Well my father's a vicar, and on Easter day every year it takes six men to carry up his money.'

\*　　\*　　\*

'Success is not always the most important thing in life,' said the preacher, 'for instance, my own great-grandfather, alas, was a very successful missionary. He was sent to an island inhabited entirely by cannibals, and he gave them their first real taste of Christianity.'

\* \* \*

A bishop, a scoutmaster and an Irishman were on board a small aeroplane when the engine caught fire. The pilot apologised for the fact that there were only three parachutes available, and that since he would be needed at the official enquiry to explain what had happened he ought to have one of them. With that he promptly strapped one on his back and jumped. The Irishman was the next to speak, explaining that as he had just won the Irish Mastermind Championship he ought to have a parachute, and he then followed the example of the pilot. At this stage the bishop spoke. 'I think you ought to have the last one,' he told the scoutmaster, 'for I am an old man who has already had the "three score years and ten" mentioned in the Bible.'

The Scoutmaster was quick to reply. 'There's no need for that, for we can each have a parachute, thank goodness. The Irish Mastermind has just jumped out with my haversack strapped to his back.'

\* \* \*

After a 'Family Day' at Chester Zoo arranged by the Mothers' Union, the local newspaper had an interesting observation: *When the open-air service finished, the bishop moved among the crowd eating their picnic sandwiches.*

\* \* \*

The curate was pleading for better relationships in the parish. 'Keep your words soft and sweet, for then they will be all the more easy to swallow if you have to eat them.'

*　　*　　*

They had never liked each other at school, and now after forty years they met on a railway platform. By this time one was a bishop, dressed in purple cassock with biretta to match. It was he who recognised the other, now an admiral in full dress uniform. The bishop couldn't resist a jibe, and going over to him asked, 'Excuse me, porter, but is this the right platform for Crewe?'

The admiral was quick on the uptake. 'Yes, it is,' he replied, 'the next train is at 3 o'clock. And then patting the bishop's considerable tummy, he added, 'but madam, are you sure you should be travelling alone in your condition?'

*　　*　　*

The church is where you go to find out what your neighbours should do to live better lives.

*　　*　　*

The new curate just couldn't remember names. His vicar gave him some good advice on the subject. He said, 'The thing to do is to pick out the most prominent feature of a person's appearance and relate it in some way to a word that rhymes with their name. For instance, when I see Mrs Parker, I remember her name because with that squashed-up nose I think of a Pekinese dog, a real barker, and that brings to mind her name Parker. Or here's another example, that man with the high cheekbones: bones brings to mind the name Jones. Mrs Davey is an untidy woman with stains on her coat – they look like gravy – so I get Davey. Do you get the idea?'

The curate thought he did, and agreed to use the system. Alas, on the very next Sunday, when the rotund Miss Jump left the church, the system failed, for instead of remembering 'plump', the curate produced the wrong cue and bade her farewell with a hearty, 'Good morning Miss Kelly.'

*　　*　　*

The newsagent flipped through a pile of newspapers searching for the *Church Times*. A customer was anxious to have his copy as soon as possible. The search was fruitless: 'I'm so sorry, but it's not here,' explained the shopkeeper, 'several other comics are also late this week.'

\*     \*     \*

'She was a perfect saint amongst women, but so dreadfully dowdy that she reminded me of a badly bound hymn book.' (Oscar Wilde)

\*     \*     \*

Mrs Roosevelt had an embroidered cushion on a settee in the White House that read: *If you can't say anything good about anybody … come and sit by me.*

\*     \*     \*

Parish magazine notice: Thursday Evenings in Lent – Pot-Luck Supper in the Hall, followed by Prayer and Medication.

\*     \*     \*

A man declined to sit on the church committee, but was good enough to explain why. He wrote, 'I believe that a committee is a collection of the unfit, chosen from among the unwilling, by the incompetent to do the unnecessary.'

\*     \*     \*

When Jock MacTavish died his widow realised the cheapest way of letting everybody hear the sad news was by a newspaper announcement. She visited the local paper and handed in her notice at the desk: it said simply, 'Jock is dead'.

The clerk said he thought that was a bit too stark and abrupt. 'And besides,' he explained, 'you are allowed six words for the same charge.'

She accepted the invitation to expand the message, and after a bit of thought handed in the new version. Now it read, 'Jock is dead, Volvo for sale'.

\*　　\*　　\*

Notice Board: WHY NOT COME IN AND GET YOUR FAITH LIFTED

\*　　\*　　\*

The young priest was soon to become vicar of a country parish, and was advised by a colleague to go and talk to some of the old men there. He was told that they could generally tell a great deal about a place. So off he went and soon discovered three of them sitting on a bench in the churchyard. To the first he asked, 'And how old are you?'

The old boy replied, 'I be 90 sir.'

'Wonderful,' said the priest, 'you don't look anything like that. What's the secret?

There was no hesitation in the reply: 'No drinking, no smoking, no women.'

The priest addressed his companion. 'What about you – what age have you got to?'

'I be 92 sir, and I am as fit as a fiddle because I keep off drink, cigarettes and women.'

It was the third man's turn now. 'I expect you are the same, aren't you, very abstemious like the others?'

'Oh no sir, not at all. I smoke 50 a day, drink 10 pints of beer a night, and I'm a terror with the women.'

'Really,' said the priest with some surprise, 'and how old are you?'

' I be 26 sir,' said the man.

\*　　\*　　\*

'He has all the delicacy of a man who sets up a fried bacon stall outside a synagogue.' (James Callaghan on a political opponent)

\*      \*      \*

The vicar said, 'This church is full of willing people - a few willing to work, and the rest willing to let them.'

\*      \*      \*

An Englishman, Irishman and Scotsman were on holiday together in Rome. Walking through the Vatican gardens one day, they were astonished to find the body of the pope, who had apparently died of a heart attack. A cardinal who was soon on the scene swore them to secrecy for a week until an official announcement could be made. They discussed it among themselves on the aeroplane on the way home, and it was the Englishman who came up with the idea of using the incident to their advantage. 'We could all go to bookmakers in our different areas, and get fantastic odds against the Pope dying within a week,' he urged, and the idea was readily accepted. They agreed to meet a fortnight later to compare results.

The Englishman turned up in a brand new Rolls Royce and explained that he had got odds of a thousand-to-one. The Scotsman arriving in his new Bentley had also made a killing with the same odds. The Irishman, however, came on his bike and sadly related that he hadn't made a penny. 'It was like this,' he said, 'I could have had a thousand-to-one like you, but to get even better odds, I doubled up the pope with the Archbishop of Canterbury.

\*      \*      \*

Church notice board: COME EARLY AND GET A SEAT AT THE BACK

\*      \*      \*

The new bishop was getting settled into the job, and his very helpful chaplain was anxious to do all he could to assist. 'You will notice, mi lord,' he said, 'that I have put on your desk a list of all the clergy of the diocese broken down by age and sex.'

*　　*　　*

Two men were in a railway carriage together. One said, 'Excuse me sir, but are you a clergyman?

'Good heavens, no!' came the reply. 'It's just that I don't feel very well.'

*　　*　　*

A vicar was bemoaning the fact that women were so much more active in parish life than men. He said he was often tempted to alter a word in the opening line of a popular hymn, and then the men could truthfully sing, *'Take my wife and let me be.'*

*　　*　　*

Old Albert used to say that it was drink and women that had killed his father. Apparently he couldn't get either, so he had shot himself!

*　　*　　*

One of the nicest families in the parish was the Robinsons – Tom and Martha and their six lovely children. It was only by chance that the vicar discovered the couple had never been married. He broached the subject very delicately. Was there, perhaps a previous marriage? Or maybe their families had objected? Or possibly they had a strong objection to the idea of marriage itself?

Martha didn't mind talking about it at all. 'Oh no, nothing like that vicar, it's on medical grounds that we never married.' When the Vicar expressed some surprise, she went on to explain, 'When I was in my teens I had a heart condition, and although I made a good recovery, the doctor was a bit cautious about the future and said that I would probably be OK if I didn't to certain things. I asked him what he meant, and after a bit of humming and hawing he said, "Well, like getting married". So Tom and me decided to play safe and just live together rather than risk damaging my health by getting married.'

\*　　\*　　\*

Many people give a tenth to the Lord – a tenth of what they ought to give.

\*　　\*　　\*

The new vicar was trying to find his way around the parish, but eventually had to stop a young man and ask the way to the post office. Having been given directions, he tried a spot of evangelism: 'Hope to see you in church on Sunday,' he said.

'Don't go to church mister,' the boy replied.

'Well, make a special effort this week, for I'm preaching on "how to get to heaven",' said the vicar.

The lad replied, 'That's rich coming from a bloke who doesn't even know where the post office is.'

\*　　\*　　\*

Vicar: 'And I warn you, I can't stand change – especially in the collection.'

\*　　\*　　\*

A Hampshire parish magazine announced, 'Saturday, July 10th, coffee morning in aid of famine relief at the vicarage.'

\*　　\*　　\*

Heckler: I wouldn't vote for you if you were the Angel Gabriel.

Political candidate: If I were the Angel Gabriel, you wouldn't be in my constituency.

\* \* \*

'He was considered a prominent churchman, mainly because of the flatness of the surrounding countryside.' (Winston Churchill on a contemporary bishop.)

\* \* \*

The Church of Ireland minister was quite surprised to be consulted by a Roman Catholic girl who lived in his area. 'You see sir,' she said, 'I am in love with a Presbyterian boy and my family will not agree to our wedding on religious grounds.' She went on, 'I thought that since you are neutral, you might be able to advise me.'

The minister thought he knew the way forward. 'I can only suggest that you try to convert your boyfriend to Roman Catholicism,' he advised.

Three months later she was back to see him again, and in obvious distress. 'Didn't you manage to do it?' he asked.

'Oh yes, I did talk him into becoming a catholic,' she sobbed, 'and in fact he started going to church with me and became very keen.'

The minister was puzzled, 'So what's the problem?' he asked.

Between the sobs the girl explained: 'Well now he's gone off to a seminary to train for the priesthood.'

\* \* \*

In the births column of a local newspaper appeared the announcement: 'To Mr and Mrs Robinson a son – a bother for Rosemary.'

\* \* \*

It was a terrible night, with a strong wind driving sleet and snow across the bleak countryside. Driving was a nightmare, but the doctor gritted his teeth and eventually made it to the isolated farmhouse on the moors. After seeing the patient he advised the wife to send at once for the vicar. He had a cup of tea in an effort to warm him up and was reluctant to face the elements again. But he was just on the point of leaving when the vicar arrived. The wet and frozen priest greeted the doctor at the door. 'Is he so very ill,' he enquired, 'do you actually think he's going to die?'

'Good gracious me no,' said the doctor, 'he'll be as right as rain in a few days, but I just didn't want to be the only one called out on a night like this.'

\*      \*      \*

The vicar meets a parishioner in the street and after the usual greeting says, 'Don't you think it's about time, Albert, that you joined the Lord's army?'

'I'm already a member of the Lord's army,' came the reply.

'If that's true, how is it that we never see you in church?'

'That's easily explained,' says Albert, 'I'm in the Secret Service.'

\*      \*      \*

From the *Tameside Reporter*: 'Stalybridge Unitarians are having a church bizarre to boost their funds.'

\*      \*      \*

The cannibal chief boasted that his people were such devout catholics that on Fridays they only ate fisherman.

\*      \*      \*

The cannibal has terrible indigestion and consults the witch doctor. He explains that on the previous day he has eaten two missionaries, and they were the type that wore hooded robes. The witch doctor asks him how he had cooked them. 'I boiled them,' he replies.

'Ah, that's where you have gone wrong,' he is told, 'you see those types are not boilers, they're friars.'

## Chapter Four

## THE BIBLE AND PRAYER

### (Or All Things Wise and Blunderful)

Tommy Cooper was for a time a soldier in one of the famous guard regiments and sometimes did sentry-duty outside the London palaces. On one such occasion, on a hot sultry day, the temptation was too great, and in the stuffy sentry box Tommy closed his eyes and went into a gentle doze. Unfortunately it was just at the time that the guard commander chose to make his inspection. When he got to within 10 yards, he barked to the sergeant-major, 'That man is asleep, arrest him immediately.'

Tommy heard the words but kept his eyes tightly shut, right up to the moment when they stamped to attention immediately in front of him. Then he opened them as wide as he could, but not before he had said one word very loudly and very distinctly – 'AMEN'.

\*     \*     \*

First Man: Sometimes I get so angry with God! I want to ask him why he allows so much misery in the world, so much cruelty, so much poverty, so much injustice, so much hunger. I am tempted to say to him, 'Why, oh why, do you allow these things to continue when you could obviously do something about it?'
Second Man: Well, why don't you?
First Man: Because I'm afraid God might ask me the same question.

\*     \*     \*

Eve was so jealous of Adam that when he came home each evening from his work in the garden she insisted on counting his ribs.

\*     \*     \*

It was only by a swift ascent up a tree that the Afro-American saved himself from the massive grizzly bear. It stood at the bottom licking its lips. Hanging on precariously to the highest branch he could reach, the frightened man said his simple prayer: 'Oh Lawd, eef you caint help me, please don't help dat grizzly bear.'

\*　　\*　　\*

At last Bernard Matthews was granted an audience with the pope. After the customary greetings, he came to the main point of the meeting. 'Your holiness, all I am asking for is a slight revision of the Lord's Prayer: instead of "Give us this day our daily bread", I want, "Give us this day our turkey leg".  There's £25,000 in it for the church if you agree.'

The pope was horrified. 'Impossible, absolutely out the question,' he said.

Bernard Matthews persisted, and in a voice little more than a whisper raised his bid. '£50,000 is my final offer,' he said.

'Done,' said his holiness, and gratefully accepted the cheque.

The next day the pope summoned the cardinals and announced the deal.  'Good news and bad news,' he told the gathering. 'You will all be pleased to know I've been given £50,000 for our funds, but the bad new is I've had to cancel the contract with Hovis.'

\*　　\*　　\*

Prayer from a devout young lady: 'Like you taught us Jesus, I am praying for others: in particular for my dear mother, that you will send her a rich and handsome son-in-law.'

\*　　\*　　\*

Once in a saintly passion
I cried with desperate grief:
'Oh Lord, my heart is black with guilt
Of sinners I am chief.'

Then stooped my guardian angel
And whispered from behind,
'Vanity, my little man,
You're nothing of the kind.'

\*　　　\*　　　\*

A lady was posting a gift of a Bible to her goddaughter. The post-office clerk examined the heavy parcel very carefully. In an officious way she asked, 'Are you sure it doesn't contain anything breakable?'

Back came the sweet reply, 'Nothing, except the Ten Commandments.'

\*　　　\*　　　\*

Surely everyone knows why God made man before he made woman. It was because he didn't want anyone standing behind him telling him how to do it.

\*　　　\*　　　\*

Value for Money

Years ago, a local artist was called in to restore a mural in the parish church and subsequently submitted a bill for £50. The parochial church council thought this was a bit steep and asked for a more detailed account. When this was received they paid without demur. It said:

| | | |
|---|---|---|
| 1. | Corrected the Ten Commandments | £5.50 |
| 2. | Embellished Pontius Pilate and put new ribbon in his bonnet | £3.40 |
| 3. | Put new tail on rooster of St Peter and mended his comb | £1.20 |
| 4. | Re-plumed and re-gilded the wings of the Guardian Angel | £7.60 |
| 5. | Washed the servant of the high priest and put carmine on his cheeks | £1.50 |

6. Renewed heaven, adjusted the stars and
   thoroughly cleaned the moon                    £10.35
7. Revived the flames of hell, put new tail on the devil,
   mended his hoof and did several odd jobs for
   the damned                                      £6.25
8. Cleaned the ears of Balaam's ass and shod him   £2.70
9. Put new stone in David's sling and deepened the
   wound in Goliath                                £4.20
10. Decorated Noah's Ark                            £5.00
11. Mended the shirt of the Prodigal Son and
    cleaned his nose                               £2.30
    Total                                          50.00

*       *       *

A man visiting the Holy Land had a sail on the Sea of Galilee.
It was a great thrill, of course, but he was a bit put out by the
high cost. He was heard to remark to a companion, 'No
wonder Jesus walked.'

*       *       *

By general agreement the vicar was the world's worst golfer.
One day on the first tee he surprised himself by hitting a
magnificent 400-yard drive. Straight down the middle it flew
before landing on the edge of the green. It started to roll the
20 yards to the hole, hit the pin and toppled in.
    The vicar was furious. He threw down his club in disgust,
stamped his foot, shook his fist, and looked up to heaven
with anger on his face and cried, 'I've told you before Lord,
cut it out, I prefer to do it myself.'

*       *       *

It wasn't the apple that caused all the trouble in the Garden
of Eden: it was the pair on the ground.

*       *       *

When Harold Macmillan, the then Prime Minister, introduced the Premium Bond Scheme, the Archbishop of Canterbury, Geoffrey Fisher, protested at the gambling element. Harold Wilson, leader of the opposition, seized upon this for political purposes. In the House of Commons he appealed to Macmillan to drop a scheme that he said would lower the moral tone of the nation. The PM in his usual sardonic fashion refused, saying, 'The members of this House will be fully aware that I am not trying to save sinners, merely trying to get sinners to save.'

\* \* \*

Teacher: Why do you think it is that in all great works of art, the inhabitants of heaven, like angels and seraphim and cherubim, always have the faces of women or young boys?
Student: Could it be that women are naturally more holy and worthy, and that men only get to heaven by a very close shave?

\* \* \*

Reuben was finally rescued from the desert island where he had been for more than 20 years since his shipwreck. Those who took him aboard their boat congratulated him on the way he had adapted to his solitary life. One said, 'How marvellous that you have been able to build such a splendid house and created such a lovely garden complete with swimming pool and summerhouse. So many other things too like the museum and the theatre. However,' he continued, 'there is one thing that puzzles me. Why on earth did you build *two* synagogues?'

Reuben replied, 'Ah well, that one over there is the one I wouldn't go to at any price.'

\* \* \*

You can tell that people who live in Paris trust in God – by the way they drive!

*     *     *

Archbishop Robert Runcie, speaking at the Free Church Federal Council annual dinner, spoke of the influence of the modern theologians C H Dodd and Reinhold Niebuhr who had both come from that wing of the church. He referred to the time when he was Principal of Cuddesdon Theological College and said, 'Those were the days when we irreverently stated that the great commandment was, "Thou shalt love the lord thy Dodd with all thy heart and thy Niebuhr as thyself".'

*     *     *

The local drunk was arguing with the vicar who was trying to reform him. The drunk said, 'A man of the cloth like you should know that the Bible teaches us that water has killed more people than whisky.'

'Where on earth does it say that?' asked the vicar.

'Have you never read about Noah and the flood?' came the reply.

*     *     *

Charlie had produced an Oscar-winning performance in court and had been awarded a quarter of a million pounds for the damage done to his back in the accident. As he left the courtroom in his wheelchair, the chief inspector from the insurance company had a quick word. 'I know you think you've fooled everybody,' he said, 'but remember, I am still watching you. From now on I'll be near you every day with my video camera, and take it from me, one day I'll get you, and then you'll be back in court for false claims and perjury.'

'That's OK with me,' replied Charlie, 'but let me tell you what you will see before too long. You will see me taken in my wheelchair to the airport. You will see them put me on board a plane bound for Lourdes. I hope you will keep your camera turned on me while I pray at the shrine, for believe me, I think you are going to see a miracle.'

\*     \*     \*

At an ecumenical gathering, three clerics were discussing the question of when life actually begins.

The RC priest had no doubts on the matter. 'It's at the moment of conception.'

The Anglican priest had a different opinion. 'It's when the baby is actually born.'

The Jewish rabbi declared they were both wrong. He said, 'Life begins when the children leave home and the dog dies.'

\*     \*     \*

The Bible tells us to love our neighbours and to love our enemies, and this is probably because they are normally the same people.

\*     \*     \*

Notice on the Spiritualist Church door: Please ring the bell, knocking only leads to confusion.

\*     \*     \*

Gerald Priestland, the BBC Religious Affairs Correspondent, met Ian Paisley in Northern Ireland. Paisley spoke first. 'And to which part of the Christian church do you belong Mr Priestland?'

'I am a Quaker,' came the reply.

'I hear the devil is a Quaker,' said Paisley.

'How so?' asked Priestland.

'When he hears the name of Jesus he quakes.'

'I have heard,' said Priestland, 'that the devil is a member of the Free Presbyterian Church.'

'How so?'

'They say the devil has all the best tunes, and I was at your hymn singing service last night.'

*     *     *

A woman and her small son are paddling in the sea at Blackpool when a great wave comes and washes the little boy out to sea. The woman is completely distraught. 'Please God,' she sobs, 'just bring him back and I'll stop swearing, stop smoking, and stop cheating at bingo.'

Another great wave appears, and miraculously the little boy is deposited by her side. After a glance at the boy the mother turns her eyes to heaven and say, 'Now Lord play the game, he did have a hat on.'

*     *     *

A Woman's Prayer: Oh Lord, please stop my neighbours from buying the things I can't afford.

*     *     *

All the animals joyfully left the ark when dry land appeared except the two snakes. Noah once more urged them to leave – 'Go forth and multiply,' he cried again. But they still refused to budge.

One of them explained, 'We can't, we're adders.'

*     *     *

'The Lord was with Joseph and he was a luckie felaw.' (Genesis 39: 2 – Tyndale translation 1530)

*     *     *

Adam and his son Abel were out taking a walk some years after being expelled from the Garden of Eden. They passed that lovely place and young Abel said, 'Look at that marvellous garden father, wouldn't it be super to live somewhere like that.'

The sad reply came, 'My boy we did actually live there once, but your mother ate us out of house and home.'

* * *

'For every difficult and complicated question there is an answer that is simple, easily understood – and wrong!' (Archbishop Habgood in General Synod)

* * *

Although we all enjoy singing, 'And did those feet in ancient times walk upon England's mountains green,' it is obvious that the gospel events could never have taken place in the British Isles. Not in England, for example, for no Jew would have been given such an exalted position as Messiah. Not in Scotland either, for any true Scot would have wanted more than 30 pieces of silver for the betrayal. And, of course, Northern Ireland is out of the question, for who would have been able to find three wise men there.

* * *

Definition: An atheist is a man who has no invisible means of support. (Fosdick)

* * *

The Lord Has Spoken!

For several years now, over 200 American cities have been targeted by the 'God Speaks' campaign. Billboards with snappy messages, allegedly from the Almighty, have lined the main roads. Here is a sample of how God is said to grab the attention of those who pass by:

*Keep using my name in vain and I'll make the rush hour longer.*
*What part of 'Thou shalt not' don't you understand?*
*Need directions? Turn right and keep straight on.*

*I know 10 things that ARE written in stone.*
*And you think it's hot here!*
*Let's meet at my house before the game on Sunday.*

\*　　　\*　　　\*

There was once an argument about which was the oldest profession. The three claimants for the title made their case.

'Obviously the medical profession is the oldest,' argued the doctor, 'for it must have been a surgeon who removed Adam's rib in order to make Eve.'

'Rubbish!' exclaimed the architect, 'for before that it was obviously a member of my profession who created order out of chaos when the world was made.'

'You are both wrong, ' boasted the politician, 'for who do you think it was that made the chaos?'

\*　　　\*　　　\*

The Old Farmer's Prayer

God bless me and my son, Ben,
Nell, my wife, and his wife Gwen.
Us four, no more, Amen.

\*　　　\*　　　\*

Nero's financial adviser urges the emperor to close the Coliseum at the earliest opportunity. 'It is just a drain on our resources,' he argued, 'the lions are eating all the prophets.'

\*　　　\*　　　\*

Adam Questions God

Why did you make Eve so beautiful?
*So that you would be attracted to her.*
Why did you give her such a sweet personality?
*So that you would fall in love with her.*
Why did you make her so stupid?
*So that she would fall in love with you.*

*   *   *

Notice in an American High School: In the event of an earthquake or tornado, the Supreme Court Ruling against prayer in schools will be temporarily suspended.

*   *   *

The famous golfer was playing a round with his friends when a severe storm broke. Thunder and lightening came in heavy doses. The other three wanted to abandon the game, recognising the danger that came from their metal clubs. But the great man would have none of it. In fact he walked into the middle of the fairway and held up high a number one iron. 'What on earth are you doing?' asked his friends in alarm. The man replied, I am letting you see that even God cannot hit a good number one iron from the fairway.'

*   *   *

Young priest talking to a doctor: Why is it that when I talk to God it's OK and we call it prayer. But when God talks to me you call it schizophrenia and want to give me pills?

*   *   *

In the midst of an argument on some point or other, Harry Cohn, the much disliked tycoon responsible for the success and ultimate fame of Columbia Pictures, once bet his brother Jack, with whom he was on very bad terms, that he could not even say the Lord's Prayer, so great was his ignorance. The wager stood at $500. Equally full of bluster, Jack Cohn accepted the bet and with a certain trepidation began, 'Now I lay me down to sleep ...'

Harry Cohn glowered and shoved the money across the table. 'That's enough,' he said, 'should have known a smart Aleck like you would come up with it.'

\* \* \*

Historians tell of one Christian emperor who was so convinced of the power of the Bible and of the need to make it part of one's life, that whenever he was ill he used to eat a few chapters, fully convinced of its potency. He died after eating the whole of the Book of Kings.

\* \* \*

'Hurray, hurray!' cried the vicar to his wife, 'this morning the postman left the gate open for the 490th time so tomorrow I can really wallop him. (Matthew18: 22)

\* \* \*

## 19th-Century Nun's Prayer

Lord, Thou knowest better than I know myself that I am now getting old. Keep me from the fatal habit of thinking I must say something on every subject on every occasion. Release me from the craving to straighten out everybody's affairs. Make me thoughtful but not moody, helpful but not bossy. With my vast store of wisdom, it seems a pity not to use it all, but Thou Lord knowest that I want a few friends left at the end.

Keep my mind free from the recital of endless details; give me wings to get to the point. Seal my lips on my aches and pains. They are increasing year by year and the love of rehearsing them is becoming sweeter as time goes by. I dare not ask for grace enough to enjoy the tales of others' woes, but help me at least to look pleasant and endure them with patience.

I dare not ask for improved memory, but for a growing humility and a lesser cocksureness when my memory seems to clash with the memories of others. Teach me the glorious lesson that occasionally I may be mistaken. Keep me reasonably sweet; I do not want to be a saint – some of them are so hard to live with – but a sour old person is one of the crowning works of the devil. Give me the ability to see good things in unexpected places, and talents in unexpected people. And give me, oh Lord, the grace to tell them so. Amen.

*   *   *

The Sunday school teacher had been stressing the poverty of the Holy Family at the time when Jesus was born. One little boy seemed unconvinced. 'Don't give me that rubbish,' he said, 'they couldn't have been all that poor to have had their portrait painted by Rubens.'

*   *   *

When a new pub was being blessed by a vicar in the new town of Runcorn, nobody knew for sure whether it was by design or accident that he used the collect for the Fourth Sunday After the Epiphany, 1928 Prayer Book:

Oh God, who knowest us to be set in the midst of so many and great dangers, that by reason of the frailty of our nature we cannot always stand upright: Grant to us such strength and protection, as may support us in all dangers, and carry us through all temptations: through Jesus Christ our Lord.

*   *   *

The Three Wise Men arrived at the stable in Bethlehem and were clearly disappointed to find the place so ordinary and poverty-stricken. The first said, 'Look at the roof, it obviously leaks.'

The second said, 'The walls are in a bad condition.'

The third said, 'OK, OK, but what did you expect, remember the place only has ONE STAR.'

*   *   *

Donald Soper, the well-known Methodist minister, often spoke from a soapbox in Hyde Park. On one occasion he was challenged by an atheist who said, 'Do you honestly expect me to believe all that rubbish in the Bible? For instance do you really think that Jonah was swallowed by a whale?'

Soper said, 'I'll ask him when I see him in heaven.'

The man retorted, 'And suppose he isn't there!'

Soper replied, 'Well, in that case, you ask him.'

\*     \*     \*

Did you hear about the agnostic, dyslexic insomniac who lies awake at night wondering if there is a dog?

\*     \*     \*

It was a great struggle for Dr Johnson to finish his dictionary, but at last the final instalment was sent to the very bad-tempered printer. Boswell tells us of the incident. The messenger finally returned, and Johnson asked him what the printer had said. 'Sir,' answered the messenger, 'he said, "Thank God I have done with him".'

'With a smile, Dr Johnson said, 'I am glad that he thanks God for anything.'

\*     \*     \*

Mark Twain was once cornered by a bore who went on and on about the after-life. 'Do you realise,' he said, 'that every time I exhale, some poor soul leaves this world and goes off into the Great Unknown.'

'Really,' replied the great man, 'have you ever tried chewing a mint?'

\*     \*     \*

A hale and hearty man in the bar is swilling down his beer with gusto. He notices a rather meek and mild man sipping lemonade in the corner. He goes over and introduces himself. 'I'm a car salesman,' he says, 'what do you do for a living?'

The second man replies with some difficulty owing to a pronounced stutter: 'I'm a s...s...s...salesman too, I s...s...sell B...B...Bibles.'

'How many Bibles do you sell in a week?' asks the first man.

'About f...f...five hundred.'

'Gosh that's marvellous: how do you do it?'

'I knock on the d...d...door, and say, "W...w...would you like to b...b...buy a B...B...Bible, or shall I r...r...read it t...t...to you".'

*     *     *

An honest prayer from a small boy: Please Lord, if you can't make me a better boy, don't worry too much about it for I'm having a pretty good time as it is.

*     *     *

God:   Noah, are you there? Ah good. I want you to build another Ark.

Noah:  Just like the first one Lord?

God:   No, rather different in fact. This one is to have ten decks, one on top of the other.

Noah:  Right Lord, no problem. Same animals?

God:   No. I don't want any animals this time, just fish. On every deck I want row upon row of fish tanks, each one full of carp. Now have you got it?

Noah:  I think so, Lord: you obviously want me to build you a MULTI-STORY CARP ARK.

*     *     *

The vicar rebuked Albert for neglecting his farm, but was given a theological explanation. 'I look at it this way your reverence,' said Albert, 'they tell me three quarters of the earth's surface is water, and so only a quarter is land. It seems to me the Good Lord is saying that a man should spend three times as much time fishing as he does ploughing.'

*     *     *

Dawn was just breaking as Lazarus, the beggar, knocked loudly on the door of Dives, the rich man, to ask for alms. Dives was furious at being got out of bed. 'How dare you disturb me at this unearthly hour?' he cried.

Lazarus replied, 'Look, do I tell you how to run your business? No. So keep your nose out of mine, OK.'

*     *     *

'Adam was the only man who when he said a good thing, knew nobody had said it before him.' (Mark Twain)

*     *     *

The church notice board had a clear invitation. It said: IF YOU ARE TIRED OF SIN – COME IN. Someone had scrawled below: IF NOT – RING CHELSEA 3303.

*     *     *

Old Matthew was out walking one day on the cliffs overlooking the sea when he slipped and fell over the edge. He managed to hang on by his fingertips, but realised he was in a perilous position, with a sheer drop of three hundred feet below him. He decided to ask for divine assistance. Looking up to heaven, he cried out, 'Help, help is there anybody there?'

Immediately an answering voice came from the clouds, 'Yes my son, I am with you. Now all you have to do is just let go, and I will send my angels to bear you gently and safely to the ground.'

There was silence for a full minute, before Matthew cried again, 'Is there anybody else there?'

*     *     *

Question: Which was the longest day in the Bible?
Answer: The day that Adam was created – for there was no Eve.

*    *    *

A man who had recently started going to church wrote an anonymous letter to the Inland Revenue saying, 'My conscience is troubling me and I can't sleep at night: please find enclosed a cheque for £1,000.' He added a PS: 'If I still can't sleep, I'll send another thousand in a few days.'

*    *    *

Airport valediction: MAY GOD AND YOUR LUGGAGE GO WITH YOU.

*    *    *

Proverbs 26: 17: 'A man who meddles with a quarrel not his own, is like a man who grabs a passing dog by its ears.'

*    *    *

Reuben's business was in dire straits and bankruptcy and disgrace stared him in the face. He went to the synagogue to plead for divine assistance. 'Please God,' he said, 'you know I have been a devout and generous member of this synagogue, but now I urgently need your help. I need to win the National Lottery as soon as possible please.'

However, he was bitterly disappointed when the results were announced, and the next day found him in the synagogue once more renewing his plea. 'Time is running out,' he prayed, 'it must be this Saturday, Lord, and do please understand I am relying on you.'

Alas, when the list of winners was published, Reuben looked in vain for his name. He was beside himself with anxiety, and didn't mince his words at his next session in the synagogue. 'You don't seem to understand, Lord,' he cried,

'I will be completely ruined unless I win the lottery – so for goodness sake, do something about it quick!'

This time there was a speedy response, and a voice from heaven said, 'OK, OK, but please, *please*, meet me half way, GO AND BUY A FLIPPIN TICKET!'

\* \* \*

In a nativity play in Wrexham, the young narrator described the scene in the stable, with Mary nursing the baby, while Joseph sat and watched the angel HOOVERING around them.

\* \* \*

An Irishman was talking to his parish priest, 'Tell me, father,' he said, 'on the day of judgement will all the Irish be present?'

'But of course, Patrick,' replied the priest.

'And the Ulstermen, father, will they be there too?'

'Certainly.'

'And what about the Scottish Presbyterians, will they be there?'

'Without doubt, they'll all be present.'

'And the English?'

'Definitely. I've told you, everybody will be there. But why are you asking all these questions?'

'Well, I was just thinking,' said Patrick, 'that maybe we shouldn't worry too much about it, for there'll be precious little judging done that first day anyway.'

\* \* \*

Church notice board: PRAYER – THE ONLY COMMODITY THAT ISN'T GOING UP.

\* \* \*

'Religion ought to refresh those parts which logic and reason cannot reach.' (Bob Langley, Pebble Mill at One presenter)

94

*　　*　　*

Goliath is obviously the biggest drunk in the whole of the Bible, for when he was up against even small things, he got himself stoned.

*　　*　　*

The Archbishop of York said in a speech that he'd recently heard a Jewish scholar explaining the making of the Sinai covenant in a typical Jewish story. God was imagined as lining up all the nations to discover who was willing to receive the Ten Commandments as His gift to mankind. The Egyptians were asked first and were a bit cagey about 'Thou shalt not kill'. The Assyrians wouldn't take 'Thou shalt not steal', and most of the nations had severe hesitations about adultery. Eventually God came to the smallest and least important of the nations and said, 'Well, you're the only ones left, so you're going to have them whether you like it or not.'

Moses only had one question. 'Are they free?'

God said, 'Yes'.

'OK,' said Moses, 'I'll have two copies.'

*　　*　　*

Isaac was very proud to live in Jerusalem and loved to take tourists round the city. He liked to tell them that this was a place specially blessed by God. 'This is obviously true,' he said to a group one day, 'you have only to look at me to see the proof of it, for when I came here I couldn't walk, couldn't feed myself, couldn't do anything for myself, and look at me now.'

One of the tourists asked, 'And when did you come here?'

'Isaac replied, 'Well, I was born here, of course.'

*　　*　　*

Question: What's the difference between Noah's Ark and Joan of Arc?

Answer: Noah's Ark was made of wood but Joan of Arc was Maid of Orleans.

\*　　\*　　\*

'A wise man knows there is only one way to make God laugh – tell Him your plans for the future.' (James Callaghan, Prime Minister 1976-79)

\*　　\*　　\*

Notice in a Whitehall office: 'giving no offence in anything, that the ministry be not blamed.' (2 Corinthians 6: 3)

\*　　\*　　\*

Mark Twain is reported as saying, 'Most people are bothered by those passages of Scripture they don't understand. But I have always noticed that the passages that bother me most are the ones I do understand!'

\*　　\*　　\*

An elderly priest introduced a personal note into the prayers at his last service before retirement. 'And if it be thy will, oh Lord, that I should lay down the office of vicar because I am growing old, then no doubt you will wish to continue to use me in an advisory capacity.'

\*　　\*　　\*

Church notice board: Make a retreat this Holy Week, and find greater peace by making contact with God (Ring 6940 2345)

\*　　\*　　\*

Father Kelly of Kelham used to say: 'No one is wholly wrong unless he thinks he is wholly right.'

\*　　\*　　\*

According to some, the most comforting words in the Bible are, *And it came ... to pass..*

* * *

Adam to Eve:   And please remember, I wear the plants in this family.

* * *

The boxing coach appeared to be a religious man for he had a text mounted on the wall of the gym where he gave his lessons. The words were from Acts 20, verse 35: HAPPINESS LIES MORE IN GIVING THAN IN RECEIVING. (NEB)

* * *

God wants spiritual fruit, not religious nuts!

* * *

Ken Dodd says he only discovered he had psychic gifts when he saw in his underpants the word *medium.*

* * *

God cannot be everywhere, that's why he made grandmothers.

* * *

It is clear from the Bible why Adam lived in Paradise – he had no mother-in-law.

* * *

The devil is the father of lies but he forgot to patent the idea.

* * *

Reuben liked to boast about the merits of his rabbi, particularly to members of a rival synagogue. 'Our splendid rabbi talks daily with the almighty,' he said one day.

'How do you know?' challenged a man from the other synagogue.

'He told me.'

'He might have been lying.'

'Nonsense! The Almighty wouldn't talk daily with a liar.'

\*     \*     \*

Question:  Who is the shortest man in the Bible?
Answer:    Bildad the Shuhite. (Job 2: ll)

\*     \*     \*

# Chapter Five

## CHILDREN, EPITAPHS AND GRACES

### (The First Flush and the Last Laugh)

Charlie was greeted warmly by St Peter when he arrived at the Pearly Gates. 'I see you have lived a very respectable life and done many good things,' said Peter, 'but before I can let you in you have to pass a spelling test.'

Charlie was taken aback, but was greatly relieved when he was told he only had to spell the word 'love'. He had no problems with it, and was quickly invited through the gates and into heaven.

'Before you go further in,' said Peter, 'would you mind doing me a favour? I have to go and see one of the angels about something, do you mind taking my place here at the gates for a few minutes?'

Charlie gladly agreed, and had no sooner sat in Peter's chair when to his great surprise the wife that he had recently left behind on earth came down the path and asked to be admitted. She was delighted to see him and explained that feeling devastated by his death, she had gone for a drive in the car, and with her mind on other things, had crashed into a tree and been killed. 'But darling,' she said, 'isn't it marvellous that we can now be together for ever and ever. We shall never be apart again. Now, just open the gates and let me in.'

'Afraid I can't do that,' said Charlie, 'the rule is that you can only come in if you pass a spelling test.'

'How very odd,' said the wife, 'but OK – what's the word I have to spell?'

Quick as a flash Charlie replied, 'CZECHOSLOVAKIA.'

\*     \*     \*

Two friends meet. One says, 'have you seen Harry lately, I've been looking high and low for him?'

The other replies, 'Well, you've been looking in the right directions, he's been dead for a fortnight.'

The Sunday school class was being questioned about the Bible. The children were reminded that in the New Testament it is written, 'No man can serve two masters'. 'Now what does this mean?' asked the teacher.

A little boy on the front row thought he knew the answer: 'Please Miss, it means a man can only have one wife.'

*     *     *

Old Yorkshire Grace

> We thank Thee Lord
> For what we've getten,
> If there'd be any moor
> It would a' bin etten.

*     *     *

There is, of course, a fence between heaven and hell. One day after a fight in hell part of it was knocked down. It lay on its side broken for many a long day in spite of repeated requests from St Peter to have it repaired. Eventually he had to threaten the devil with legal action if it were not put right soon. Sadly, the devil laughed in his face, saying, 'I'm not afraid of your threats. Legal action, you say, and where do you think you'll be able to get a lawyer!'

*     *     *

Howlers

Question: What do you know about the pope?
Answer: He lives in a vacuum.
Question: What punishment did God mete out to Adam for being disobedient?
Answer: He expelled him from Eton.
Question: Who is the patron saint of travellers?

Answer:     St Francis of the Sea Sick.

Question:   What did St Paul do when the people of
            Macedonia would not believe the gospel?

Answer:     He got stoned.

\*       \*       \*

The old Duke of Norfolk was called on to say grace at a
dinner. As the kingdom's senior Roman Catholic layman he
was not content with one of the traditional well-known
prayers, but began composing his own thanksgiving. He was
well launched into his second paragraph, 'For all thy great
and merciful bounty, oh Lord, we thy humble servants
gathered here today do give unto thy gracious majesty ...'

At this point there came an interruption, then a loud
voice from the back of the hall called out, 'Speak up, please,
I can't hear you.'

The Duke looked at him austerely over his glasses and in
an icy tone replied, 'I am not talking to YOU.'

\*       \*       \*

They say you can't take it with you but there was no
mistaking the glee with which the congregation concluded
the final hymn at the bank manager's funeral. 'Guide me oh
thou great redeemer,' they sang, but it was the misprint in
the last verse that kindled their hope and enthusiasm as they
bellowed, 'land my safe on Canaan's side'.

\*       \*       \*

A Solicitor's Grace

> For good food and friends and all that we see
> We thank you Lord as we make our strong plea;
> A plea for firm wills to preserve us from folly,
> With last-minute codicils to bring in more lolly.
> And preserve us from clients both rude and fickle,
> But do please ensure, Lord, a nice steady trickle.

Keep us, we beg you, in courtly sobriety,
A credit, each one, to the great Law Society.
And finally, Lord, when our short lease is run,
May we look back and hope that we've not missed the fun.
OYEZ: OYEZ:    OYEZ!

*    *    *

Oscar Wilde said the only way to get rid of temptation was to give in to it. A very different line came from a schoolboy who said, 'When I go past a strawberry field I can't stop my mouth watering, but I can run!'

*    *    *

The multi-millionaire had arranged every detail of his own funeral. It was to be in Miami, and instead of a coffin he was to be placed inside his gold-plated Cadillac. When the day came, his instructions were followed to the letter, and dressed in a white tuxedo, he was put into his beautiful motorcar in the appointed place. A huge hole had been dug in the ground, and a crane hoisted the car into the air above it, all ready for the drop. A crowd of sightseers gathered, and one of them was heard to say, 'Gee, now that's what I call livin'.'

*    *    *

A curious epitaph on a pottery-worker's grave is found in a churchyard in Chester.

Beneath this stone lies Catherine Gray,
Changed to a lifeless lump of clay;
By earth and clay she got her pelf
And now she's changed to earth herself.
Ye weeping friends, let me advise,
Abate your years and dry your eyes:
For what avails a flood of tears?

Who knows, but in a course of years,
In some tall pitcher or brown pot
She may once more be in her shop.

*     *     *

The three kings in the primary school nativity play made their entry with great pomp and style. The first came to the manger and with a flourish declared, 'I bring gold.' The second king hesitated and to end an embarrassing silence the third king stepped in with, 'And I bring Myrrh.' By this time the second king had almost remembered his lines and in a loud voice said, 'And Frank sent this.'

*     *     *

A Yorkshire Grace

Stick in, till ye stick out. Amen

*     *     *

An Englishman, an Irishman and a Scotsman were asked what they would do if their doctor told them they had only six months to live. The Englishman said, 'I would put my affairs in order, make a will, and retire to the peace and quiet of the country to await my end.'

The Irishman said, 'Since I have no close relatives, I would sell everything I own and really live it up for six months – best hotels, best food and drink – paint the town red.'

The Scotsman had a much better answer. He said, 'I would get a second opinion.'

*     *     *

Some parents have difficulty finding a name for the new baby: others have a rich relative!

*　　　*　　　*

While putting her five-year-old daughter to bed one evening, a mother read her the story of the Prodigal Son. They discussed how the young son had taken his inheritance and left home, living it up until he had nothing left. Finally, when he couldn't even eat as well as the pigs, he returned home to his father, who welcomed him with love and forgiveness. When they finished the story, the mother asked her daughter what she had learned from it. After thinking for a moment, she replied. 'Well mummy, I think it means you should never leave home without your Goldfish.' (For the uninitiated, Goldfish = credit card.)

*　　　*　　　*

Heavenly Father, bless our plate,
And keep us in a happy state:
Bless the cook and all who serve us.
From upset stomachs, Lord preserve us.

*　　　*　　　*

Famous last words: 'Die, dear doctor, die! That's the last thing I shall do.' (Lord Palmerston, died in office as Prime Minister, 1865)

*　　　*　　　*

A true story from the Methodist church in Buckingham tells how the preacher one Sunday took as his theme, 'The Love of God.' In his introduction he stressed how having God as our Father made us all brothers and sisters, and made possible our close relationship, one with another. After this he asked the children a question. 'What is it that binds us all together?' A young voice on the front row called out the answer - 'SKIN'.

A priest tells how disconcerted he was recently by the choice of music at the crematorium where he was on duty. It was said to be the deceased's favourite hymn but that still didn't make it any more appropriate – 'Give me oil in my lamp, keep me burning'.

It must have been the priest's unlucky day, for at the very next funeral an hour later, the service ended (again by special request) with a recording of Elvis Presley singing, 'Return to sender, address unknown'.

*     *     *

Susie was a sweet little girl, pink cheeked, blue-eyed, blonde hair, a real poppet, and everybody adored her. However, she had one grave fault that worried her mother no end – she told fibs, real porkies! One day she arrived home from school with the news that she had seen a great lion standing by the bus shelter. Her mother reprimanded her and gradually got her to admit that she had exaggerated a perfectly normal incident, and that she had in fact just seen a rather large dog. Susie was told that when she said her prayers that night she should tell God how sorry she was for having said such a thing. Later that evening, mother went upstairs to say goodnight to her daughter and asked whether she had done it.

'Oh yes, mummy,' came the reply, 'I told God I was very sorry, and do you know what He said back to me? He said, "Don't worry Susie, I often get mixed up with dogs and lions myself".'

*     *     *

IN LOVING MEMORY OF JANE HARRISON

Gone to be an angle

Food and folk, oh Lord, please bless,
And grant our guests we may impress:
Let it seem this is the way
We dine and entertain each day:
And let the daily woman stay
Long as it takes to clear away.

*     *     *

Alas, the man had arrived in hell. But at least he was to be
given some choice as to how he would spend eternity. He was
shown round the place and the various options were put to
him. The first was very much as he expected, with the lost
souls labouring in the boiler-house, stoking the fires in
extreme temperatures, perspiration rolling down their
cheeks. The next place seemed even worse, for here the
junior devils were busy whipping and torturing the victims
as they writhed and screamed. It was with some relief that
they moved to the third and final option. Here the damned
stood up to their shoulders in slimy, steaming mud, but at
least they were all drinking mugs of tea. Without hesitation
the man made it plain that this was where he wanted to be.
He stripped off, jumped into the mud, and was handed his
cup of tea. Unfortunately he only had time for one sip before
the command rang out, 'OK - TEA BREAK OVER - BACK
ON YOUR HEADS!'

*     *     *

A firm of funeral directors boasted that it was able to provide
customised funerals and gave examples of recent successes
in this field. These included:

A binman: He was cremated, and his ashes scattered up and
down the path of every house in the avenue, with
every gate left open.

A pornographer: His coffin was wrapped in plain brown
paper, and the mourners stood with eyes

averted, pretending to watch something else in a different part of the cemetery.

A solicitor: His funeral was much the same as anybody else's except there were two collections instead of the usual one, and the hymn, 'Take my silver and my gold' was sung.

An escapologist: His funeral was held on June 18, 20, 22, and 24 …

A vicar: At his funeral the bishop came and celebrated, and it took six of the local clergy to carry the bier.

\*     \*     \*

Children's Names For God

Father Witchart in heaven: Lead us not into Thames Station, Harold be they name
Thanks Peter God for giving us the Prairie Tortoise.

\*     \*     \*

A Bishop of Winchester aboard a yacht during Cowes week was asked to say grace before lunch. He came out with, 'In view of the weather forecast that we have just heard on the one o'clock news, I can only say: For what we may be allowed to retain, may the Lord make us truly thankful.'

\*     \*     \*

When Winston Churchill celebrated his 90th birthday he was asked how he felt.

'Fine' he replied, 'especially when you consider the alternative.'

\*     \*     \*

Shortest Grace On Record

Heavenly Pa, ta.

*     *     *

A mother and her little boy were staying at a cottage in the country. Since there was no electricity, they had to rely on candles for lighting. The first night there, as they were climbing the stairs on the way to bed, a draught of wind blew out the candle, leaving them in total darkness. Mother said, 'Don't worry, just stand here and I will go down for the matches, and remember, Jesus is with you.'

The little boy thought for a moment and then replied, 'I've got a better idea mummy, you stay here with me, and send Jesus for the matches.'

*     *     *

IN MEMORY OF RUFUS THE GOAT - REGIMENTAL MASCOT

> Who in his time kicked
> Two colonels
> Five majors
> Eight captains
> Sixteen lieutenants
> Forty sergeants
> Over a hundred privates
> And one landmine

*     *     *

Mary had been a very devout, churchgoing Yorkshire woman, and when she eventually died her husband thought he had the perfect epitaph. He instructed the mason to carve the words, *SHE WAS THINE* on her tombstone. When the work was done he went to inspect it, and found to his horror that the mason had made a mistake and the message read, *SHE WAS THIN*. He hurriedly summoned the mason and angrily told him, 'You silly man, you have missed off the 'E', I want it putting right immediately.' It was agreed the man would go back later in the day to see the correction. Alas, on his return he was even more horrified to see that the inscription now read, *'EE, SHE WAS THIN.'*

*       *       *

Hodges Grace

Lord bless each one although a sinner,
And help us stay alive;
There's ten of us for dinner,
And not enough for five.

*       *       *

There are two sets of people who are never tired of telling you that there are better places to be than where you are now, namely, estate agents and preachers!

*       *       *

When an elderly lawyer was told by his doctor that he was terminally ill, he rushed home and began frantically to leaf through the Bible. He told his wife he was looking for loopholes.

*       *       *

Tommy's mother heard him praying very earnestly one night asking for a new bike. He finished by saying, 'Send it this week and I will be kind to everybody for the rest of the month.'

She rebuked her son for trying to bargain with God but it did little good, for a few nights later he was on the same tack, and she heard him saying, 'This is my last offer Jesus, a new bike this week and I'll be good for three months.'

Again she told him off, even more strictly then before. Later that week she was cleaning out the cellar, and was surprised to find a statue of the Virgin Mary hidden under some old cardboard boxes in a corner. Normally it had pride of place on a table in the sitting room. She guessed her son had something to do with its removal to the cellar, and rushed up to his room to question him on the subject. He was not there, but she did discover a note on the windowsill which said, 'Dear Jesus, You know what you have to do if you want to see your mother again.'

*     *     *

After a glass of whisky too many, the man is boasting of his family background. 'For five generations my family has followed the medical profession,' he says.

'You mean they were all doctors,' says the barman.

'Certainly not, they were all undertakers,' came the reply.

*     *     *

Overheard in Heaven

'Clever man, my doctor, he was absolutely right. Said I would be out of hospital in a fortnight.'

*     *     *

He got into heaven without any difficulty, but looked rather anxious as he scanned the faces of the other arrivals. St Peter was curious so he explained why he was so interested in the new entrants. 'I would rather like to meet again the last person I saw before I died,' he explained, 'for we shared a few ups and downs. It was like this, I jumped out of an aeroplane on a sponsored parachute jump and the wretched thing failed to open. I was on my way hurtling to the ground when I passed a fellow with a spanner in his hand coming up as fast as I was going down. I called to him, "Do you know anything about parachutes?"

'He shouted back, "No, and to be honest, I don't know much about gas cookers either".'

*     *     *

Two little boys stood on the doorstep waiting for their friend to finish his lunch before having a game of football. One says, 'His mother must be a terrible cook.'

'Why?' asks his mate.

'They say a prayer before every meal.'

*   *   *

In The Pet's Cemetery

In Loving Memory of Blackie
His Barque is On Another Shore

*   *   *

Geoffrey Fisher's *Grace of Disapproval* at Repton School: 'For what we are about to receive, and for what some have already snatched, may the Lord make us truly thankful.'

*   *   *

Rushing from one thing to another can present problems for a priest, and sometimes means inadequate preparation, as one particular vicar realised one day when he started a funeral service without having had time to get the details of the deceased. In fact he didn't even know whether it was a man or a woman he was burying, but he did know that in the next prayer he had to refer to either 'our dear departed brother' or 'our dear departed sister', so he leaned across to a man in the front pew and whispered, 'Brother or sister?'

Back came the reply, 'No. Just a good friend.'

*   *   *

A little girl was taken to church by her grandfather, when it was time for the collection he was given some advice by the diminutive figure at his side. In a loud whisper she instructed him, 'Don't pay for me, granddad, I'm under five.'

*     *     *

Here lies the body of Mary Jones,
Who died of eating cherry stones;
Her name was Smith, it was not Jones,
But Jones was put to rhyme with stones.

*     *     *

Howlers From a Lancashire School

Circumcision has always been a sore point with the Jews.
What were t'ducks about they didna swim. (After a lesson on
Noah and the flood)

*     *     *

The new curate was trying very hard with his first funeral
sermon. Pointing to the coffin, he said, 'There is left here
only the shell ... the nut has gone to heaven.'

*     *     *

The sign said: WELCOME TO ISRAEL, A MECCA FOR
TOURISTS

*     *     *

Advertisement in a Yorkshire paper: 'Secondhand
tombstone for sale: would suit family called Grundy'.

*     *     *

A young and enthusiastic Salvation Army Officer was on her
rounds in the pubs selling the *War Cry* and collecting for the
local citadel. When the tin she was passing round came to
old Ted, he asked her what the money was for. 'It's for the
Lord,' she proclaimed.

'Well, in that case you'd better give it to me love,' said the old chap, 'for I reckon I'll be seeing Him afore you.'

\*　　\*　　\*

The four of them had been friends since schooldays, and now sadly they gathered at the home of one prior to his funeral. It was to be conducted by another of them who was a priest. He said some prayers in the house before their departure for the church. And then just before they left, they knew there was a ritual they had to perform in accordance with a tradition in the deceased's family. Apparently it was normal for dear and close friends to place a gift in the coffin before the final leave-taking. The three friends had agreed to give £100 each. The first stepped forward and put his cash in the coffin: the second did likewise. The priest quickly wrote out a cheque for £300, put it in the coffin and pocketed the cash.

\*　　\*　　\*

A small girl was taken to her first wedding ceremony. She thought it was marvellous and very exciting. But one thing puzzled her. She asked, 'Mummy, why did the bride change her mind at the last minute, for she came in with one man and then went out with another? But I did like the second one best.'

\*　　\*　　\*

Here lies the body of Thomas Mound
Lost at sea, and never found.

\*　　\*　　\*

An advertisement from a firm of undertakers says, 'Death is an event most people only have to cope with occasionally in their lives.'

*    *    *

In A Country Churchyard

Sacred to the memory of Thomas Anderson
Who died in Philadelphia, March 1753
Had he lived he would have been buried here.

*    *    *

A little boy is busy drawing a picture. The teacher asks, 'And what is that going to be?'
The boy replies, 'I'm drawing God.'
'But nobody knows what God looks like', said the teacher.
'They will when I've finished,' comes the reply.

*    *    *

From Scotland comes this true story. The minister's theme centred on 'the Temptations', in illustrating it he said, 'If someone said to you that you could have anything in the world that you wanted, what would you say?'
Breaking the silence, a five-year-old boy at the front said, 'Thank you.'

*    *    *

Here lies Solomon Peas
Under the trees and sod;
But Peas is not here,
Only the pod,
For Peas is shelled out and is gone to God.

*    *    *

Question:  Why do they build walls around cemeteries?
Answer:    Because people are dying to get in.

*    *    *

'For myself, the only immortality I desire is to invent a new sauce.' (Oscar Wilde)

* * *

## A Salutary Epitaph

I had the right of way, but the other guy had the truck.

* * *

A little girl was praying just before Christmas. 'Please God, I would love to have a little baby brother.' To her great surprise and delight her mother returned home on Christmas Eve with a baby boy in her arms.

The following year the little girl prayed again. 'Please God, if it wouldn't be too uncomfortable for mummy, this time I'd like a pony.'

* * *

Notice Board: For those of you who have children and don't know it we have a nursery downstairs.

* * *

The Chairman of British Airways went to heaven. He knocked at the pearly gates, which were opened by a rather testy St Peter. 'Come in, come in, quickly now: sit over there,' said Peter, 'we're expecting an important visitor! In a short while there came through the gates the smartly uniformed figure of a British Airways Captain. Trumpets blew, cherubim and seraphim fluttered about. Angels and archangels bowed low.

The chairman was incensed. 'Look here,' he cried, 'this is ridiculous: I am the Chairman of British Airways and here I am sitting out in the cold while you make all this fuss about a British Airways Captain.'

'Ah,' said Peter, 'you don't quite understand: that is in fact God, he only thinks he is a British Airways Captain.'

*     *     *

## A Commercial Epitaph

Beneath this stone in hope of Zion
Doth lie the landlord of 'The Lion'.
Resigned unto the heavenly will,
His son keeps up the business still.

*     *     *

In a Dublin school, a priest was questioning the children on their knowledge of history. 'Who was the greatest man who ever lived?' he asked. There was no reply, so to encourage concentration he added an inducement: 'Whoever gives me the right answer will get a shilling.' This made several children decide to have a go.

'Abraham Lincoln,' said one.

'Julius Caesar,' volunteered another.

'Saint Patrick,' called out a little Jewish boy.

He was given the shilling, and the priest congratulated him.

'Thank you father,' said the boy, 'I knew the right answer was Moses, but business is business.'

*     *     *

Rub-a-dub-dub
Thank God for the grub:
And eeny, meeny, miny, mo,
Bless the booze and let it flow.

*     *     *

A vicar from the Chester diocese recounts the true story of an unusual happening at a funeral he was taking. The deceased was a man who rarely entered the church but who was a well-known character in the village, and a regular customer at one of the local pubs. As the vicar completed the committal at the

116

graveside, a friend of the dead man stepped forward and took three darts from his pocket which he proceeded to throw very expertly into the lid of the coffin, saying, 'Them's the things he liked best of all, and if he's on double-top now, that'll be his bullseye.' The vicar thought it a not inappropriate epitaph.

\* \* \*

Bless this food, we pray, oh Lord
Bless the folk around the board,
We'll eat and eat till pain is felt
Then find relief with a notch of the belt.

\* \* \*

A little boy was sent by his mother to the corner shop to buy some washing-up liquid. By the time he got there he had forgotten the name of it. He said to the shopkeeper, 'Please can I have some of that stuff that God uses.' The shopkeeper was mystified. He asked for more details. 'Well,' said the boy, I think it's called *Innus*, because we say in church, "Oh God make clean our hearts with in us".'

\* \* \*

I dreamt death came the other night and heaven's gate swung wide,
An angel with a halo bright invited me inside:
And there to my astonishment were folk I'd judged and labelled
As quite unfit, of little worth, and spiritually disabled.
Indignant words rose to my lips but never were set free,
For every face showed stunned surprise – no one expected ME!

\* \* \*

Thank you Lord for this very fine dinner,
If it wasn't for you, we'd all be much thinner.

*       *       *

A man gets to the gates of heaven. St Peter asks him his occupation. 'I'm a scrap-metal dealer,' says the man. Peter says he will have to go and ask God if he can enter, for 'to be honest, we are not very keen on having members of your profession here.' He comes back in ten minutes and the man has disappeared – so too have the gates.

*       *       *

A much quoted epitaph on Andrew Meekie's grave from Carry, near Edinburgh:

Beneath these stones lie Meekie's bones,
O Satan, gin ye take him:
Gie him the schoolin o' your weans
And clever devils he'll make 'em.

*       *       *

The solicitor making the will was intrigued by one of the requests. 'But why do you want your ashes to be scattered over Harrods?' he asks.

The woman explained, 'It's just to make sure that my daughter visits me at least once a week.'

*       *       *

In Holmer churchyard, Hereford, it would appear the mason did not have sufficient space to complete the text, (Proverbs 12: 4) so he expressed the words 'a crown' symbolically, and this we read:

'A virtuous woman is 5s to her husband'

*       *       *

The lesson had been on the name of Jesus. They were soon going to end Sunday school with the hymn, 'How sweet the name of Jesus sounds'. But before that the teacher asked a last question. 'What is our favourite word? What word do we Christians like to call out better than any other?'

A little girl answered with no hesitation. 'Please Miss, it's bingo, bingo.'

*　　*　　*

Old Irish Blessing

And may you get to heaven before the devil knows you're dead.

*　　*　　*

Confirmation candidate to the vicar: 'I really don't see any need to say my prayers every night. There are some nights when I don't need anything.'

*　　*　　*

This is a true story about Frank, an undertaker's assistant. He had to take the hearse some 200 miles to pick up a body from a hospital mortuary. On the way back, he was tired enough to pull into a lay-by for a short rest and a cup of coffee from his thermos flask. There were already several vehicles in the lay-by, and the only space for Frank was alongside a large articulated lorry, the driver of which was obviously fast asleep with his head resting on his arms on the steering wheel. As Frank leaned back and enjoyed his coffee, the lorry driver woke up with a start and eyed with obvious alarm the hearse and its cargo alongside. Then opening his window and motioning Frank to do the same, he called out, 'I'll tell you what mate, you're in a bit of a hurry aren't you, I was only having forty winks.'

*　　*　　*

The lesson had been on David slaying Goliath with a stone from his sling. The children had been spellbound. 'And now,' said the teacher, 'what does this story teach us?'

'Please Miss,' answered Johnny, 'it teaches us to duck.'

\*     \*     \*

From a churchyard in Ripon, Yorkshire

Here lies poor, but honest, Bryan Tunstall,
He was a most expert angler:
Until death, envious of his mart,
Threw out his line and hooked him,
And landed him here, the 21ˢᵗ day of April 1790.

\*     \*     \*

'Please God, send me a computer and lots of games to go with it for my birthday, please, please, please,' pleaded Tommy as he knelt in the living room and said his evening prayers.

'There is no need to shout,' said his mother, 'God is not deaf.'

'No, but grandma is, and she's right over there in the corner.'

\*     \*     \*

Newspaper notice: The funeral service will be followed by a private cremation for the immediate family.

\*     \*     \*

The horse bit the parson:
How came that to pass?
The horse heard the parson say
'All flesh is grass'.

\*     \*     \*

120

The scene is the gate of heaven. A man knocks and asks for admission. St Peter scrutinises the records, and then sternly addresses the applicant. 'I am afraid you cannot come in,' he says, 'for I see from your file that you have lived a very wicked and selfish life. You are obviously arrogant, selfish and proud, and there is no place for you here.'

The man protests vigorously, 'Look here, you appear to have overlooked one thing. Just before I died, I actually gave £10,000 to Oxfam, and was given to understand that such generosity would not go unrewarded in the afterlife. Now what do you say to that?'

For a moment St Peter seemed at a loss, but then promised to look into the matter, and he asked the man to come back in an hour. At the appointed time when the man reappeared, Peter handed him an envelope. 'Take this,' he said, 'we've had a whip-round among the angels, and here is your ten grand - now buzz off.'

\*     \*     \*

'Dad, did you go to Sunday school when you were a boy?'

'Yes, my boy, every week as regular as clockwork.'

'That settles it. I'm giving it up. It's not doing me any good either.'

\*     \*     \*

It was a frosty morning, and people at the crematorium had difficulty walking on the paths which were covered with ice. 'Please walk carefully,' advised the undertaker to his funeral party, 'wouldn't you think they would get some ashes for the place.'

\*     \*     \*

The class of young children had revelled in the exciting story of Jonah being swallowed by a whale. There had been lots of 'oohs' and 'aahs', but the moral had still to be drawn. 'Now children, think carefully, what does this story teach us?'

One little boy had no doubts at all. 'Please Miss, it teaches us that you can't keep a good man down.'

* * *

Epitaph in Peterborough Cathedral – in memory of Jane Parker, midwife, 1653:

> Here lieth a midwife, brought to bed,
> Deliveress Delivered:
> Her body being churched here,
> Her soul gives thanks in yonder sphere.

* * *

'When the angels play music for God they play Bach: when they play for themselves they play Mozart.' (Archbishop Robert Runcie)

* * *

An Englishman took his friend Paddy for a walk through the cemetery. They came to a tombstone which read:

> HERE LIES ANGUS MACTAVISH
> A KIND AND GENEROUS MAN
> AND A LOVING FATHER

'Will yez look at that.' said Paddy, 'now isn't that just like the Scots, burying three men in one grave.'

* * *

A story from Lancashire, said to be true, tells of a shy and nervous curate who was greatly relieved when he managed to get through his first funeral service without a hitch. Rather reluctantly he accepted an invitation back to the house afterwards for the customary repast. The newly bereaved widower was anxious to put him at his ease, and quickly put a cup of tea into his hands. He then reappeared with a plate covered with slices of fruitcake. Pushing it under the curate's nose he said, 'Come on lad, 'ave a piece o' this: made with the corpse's own hand.'

* * *

Three children in the playground were boasting about their fathers. One said, 'My daddy is a teacher, and he makes us clever for nothing.'

The next said, 'My daddy is a doctor, and he makes us better for nothing.'

The third said, 'My daddy is a vicar, and he makes us good for nothing.'

* * *

A man was in his garden digging a hole. A neighbour pokes his head over the fence and asks him what he is doing. 'I'm digging a grave for the budgie,' he says.

The neighbour says, 'That's rather a large hole for a budgie, isn't it?'

The man replies, 'Of course, but it is inside your cat.'

* * *

An epitaph from Cheltenham:

Here lies John Higgs,
A famous man for killing pigs
For killing pigs was his delight,
Both morning, afternoon, and night:
Both heats and colds he did endure,
Which no physician e'er could cure,
His knife is laid, his work is done,
I hope to heaven his soul is gone.

* * *

Little boy saying his prayers: 'Dear God, I'm afraid this really is goodbye: tomorrow we move to Liverpool.'

\* \* \*

Two Scots meet on the steps of the kirk. Says one, 'Maun Jamie, do you ken Angus is deed?'

'No man, d'ye tell me!'

'Aye, deed and buried. An' he left forty thoosan' pounds.'

'No man, you're wrang there: kennin Angus, he wouldna *leave* it. He'd ha to be dragged frae it!'

\* \* \*

Here lies the body of Jonathan Hyde
Fell down a midden and grievously died,
Albert his brother fell down another,
Cleansed now by Grace, they lie side by side.

\* \* \*

The Sunday school class was asked, 'What is the last book in the Bible? The child who answered spoke more wisely than she realised when she said, 'The Book of Revolution'.

\* \* \*

Grace At Breakfast

This is the day the Lord hath made: Give thanks for toast and marmalade.

\* \* \*

Should she have gone to realms above,
Farewell to peace and heavenly love,
But if she's sought the lower level,
The Lord have mercy on the devil.

*　　*　　*

The little boy got lots of lovely gifts for Christmas. There was a machine gun, a stealth bomber, a combat outfit, and a nuclear submarine. And they were all wrapped up in lovely paper that said, *Peace on Earth And Goodwill Amongst Men.*

*　　*　　*

The little girl sat on her grandad's knee with her ear pressed closely against his chest. She was obviously listening intently to his breathing. She explained, 'Try to make a noise like a frog grandad, for I heard mummy say to daddy yesterday that when you have croaked we'll be able to have a good holiday.'

*　　*　　*

A Lawyer's Grace
　　For whom we are about to deceive,
　　May the Lord make us truly thankful.

A Glutton's Grace
　　Lord, may we eat all we are able.
　　Until our stomachs touch the table.

A Hungry Man's Grace
　　For each and every plateful,
　　May the Lord make us truly grateful.

*　　*　　*

The funeral was a very sad occasion for the farmer's mother-in-law had been savaged by a cow, normally such a placid and docile animal. The whole farming community came to the service, and afterwards the vicar remarked on the splendid turnout to the knowledgeable old verger.

'Don't get the wrong idea,' said the old man, 'they were not here today out of respect, they really came to make a bid for the cow.'

    \*       \*       \*

Here lies the body of Mary Ann,
Who rests in the bosom of Abraham.
It's all very well for Mary Ann.
But what about poor old Abraham.

    \*       \*       \*

The text in that part of the vestry used as a baby crèche during the Sunday services came from St Paul – 1 Corinthians 15: 51 – 'We shall not all sleep, but we shall all be changed.'

    \*       \*       \*

A little boy is saying his prayers. He asks for blessings on mummy and daddy, on grandad and grandma, and on everybody he can think of. At the end he concludes with, 'Oh yes God, and please remember to look after yourself, for if anything happens to you we're all sunk.'

    \*       \*       \*

From a gravestone in North Wales

Here lies the mother of children seven,
Three on earth and four in heaven:
The four in heaven preferring rather
To die with mother than live with father.

    \*       \*       \*

Alexander Pope (1688-1744) in one of his 'Moral Essays' describes how Euclio dictates his will to an attorney:
    'I give and I bequeath,' old Euclio said, 'my lands and tenements to Ted.'
    'The money sir?'
    'Must it be all? Oh very well, I give it Paul.'
    'The manor?'

'The manor: Hold!' he cried, 'I cannot part with that' ...
and died.

* * *

'Tell me what you know about God,' began the Sunday
school teacher. There was a quick response from a little girl
on the front row. 'God is the man who saved the Queen.'

* * *

Mother-in-Law to Geordie: Aad love t'dance on thy grave
when thou dees.
Geordie to Mother-in-Law: Aa hope tha dis for A want to be
buried at sea.

* * *

The village school decided to move up-market a bit by giving
itself a motto. The most popular suggestion was, 'I hear, I
see, I learn'. Not surprisingly, the majority of the pupils
voted for it to be in Latin, for they liked the sound of 'Audio,
Video, Disco'.

* * *

Epitaph on a cricketer's grave:

   I bowl'd, I struck, I caught, I stopped,
   Sure, life's a game of cricket:
   I blocked with care, with caution popp'd
   Yet death has hit my wicket.

* * *

Epitaph on a brewer's grave in Jersey, Channel Islands

   Here lies poor Burton
   He was both Hale and Stout:
   Death laid on him his bitter bier,
   Now in another world he hops about.

*　　*　　*

Old Charlie the bookie died, and two tick-tack men who were his friends joined the congregation for the funeral service at the Roman Catholic church. Both were better versed in matters of the turf than in things ecclesiastical, and as they were a bit apprehensive about the proceedings, they sat well at the back. When the priest came in and made the sign of the cross over himself, one of the tick-tack men turned to his companion in alarm and whispered, 'Oh dear, things look black for Charlie, he seems to be starting at a hundred to one.'

*　　*　　*

The bishop made his chaplain promise that when he died there would be inscribed on his headstone the plaintive words, *GONE TO ANOTHER MEETING*.

*　　*　　*

The vicar played golf once a week with old Bill, the verger. In spite of his advanced years and his rheumatics Bill always won. After yet another defeat, the vicar complained, 'No matter how well I play you always manage to beat me. I reckon the only time I am ever going to win is when I stand over your grave and take your funeral.

With a toothless grin, the old man replied, 'Aye, and even then it'll be my hole.'

*　　*　　*

The widow had a rather strange request for the undertaker after her husband's funeral. She explained, 'He was a very slipshod DIY man, and that's why I want his tombstone to be lopsided and bearing the words, IT'LL DO.'

*　　*　　*

128

In his prayers one night, little Tommy made an unusual plea to the Almighty: 'Oh God will you please put Birmingham into Lancashire – I've said it's there in an exam at school today.'

*     *     *

An epitaph in Wolstanton, Staffordshire:

In Memory of Ann Jennings
Some have children, some have none,
Here lies the mother of twenty-one

*     *     *

The 30-year-old lawyer was furious with St Peter. 'A heart attack at my age,' he screamed, 'surely you've made a terrible mistake.'

Peter agreed to go and check the records. He was back soon, full of apologies. 'I am so very sorry,' he said, 'but our calculations were based on your billable hours, and we had you down to be at least 120 years old.'

*     *     *

A memorial to Rebecca Freeland of Edwalton, Nottinghamshire who died in 1741 says:

She drank good ale, good punch and wine,
And lived to the age of 99.

*     *     *

The grace of Robert Herrick (1591-1674:

God to my little meal and oil
Add but a little flesh to boil,
And thou my pipkinnet shalt see
Give a wave offering to thee.

(pipkinnet = earthenware pot or pan)

\*     \*     \*

Here lies the body of William Gray
Who died defending his right of way:
He was right, of course, right all along,
But he's just as dead as if he'd been wrong.

\*     \*     \*

Old golfers never die, they simply lose their drive:
Old teachers never die, they simply lose their class:
Old lawyers never die, they simply lose their appeal:
Old vicars never die, they simply lose their living.

\*     \*     \*

# INDEX